Benedikt Budig

Extracting Spatial Information from Historical Maps

Benedikt Budig

Extracting Spatial Information from Historical Maps

Algorithms and Interaction

Würzburg
University Press

Dissertation, Julius-Maximilians-Universität Würzburg
Fakultät für Mathematik und Informatik, 2017
Gutachter: Dr. Thomas C. van Dijk, Prof. Dr. Alexander Wolff, Prof. Dr. Yao-Yi Chiang
Diese Arbeit wurde durch ein Promotionsstipendium der Studienstiftung des deutschen Volkes unterstützt.

Impressum

Julius-Maximilians-Universität Würzburg
Würzburg University Press
Universitätsbibliothek Würzburg
Am Hubland
D-97074 Würzburg
www.wup.uni-wuerzburg.de

© 2018 Würzburg University Press
Print on Demand

Coverdesign: Julia Bauer
Karte: UB Würzburg, 36/A 10.12

ISBN 978-3-95826-092-4 (print)
ISBN 978-3-95826-093-1 (online)
URN urn:nbn:de:bvb:20-opus-160955

Preface

This book is concerned with the extraction of spatial information from historical documents, mostly from maps. This puts it at a crossroads of various disciplines – computer science, geographic information science, digital humanities – and Benedikt Budig navigates this intersection with clarity, combining a keen algorithmic eye with an affinity for the historical material. In a way, the book itself functions like a map: it provides an overview of this area of research by showing you a selection of interesting places it contains, and how to get there.

The first two chapters give an overview of the research goals, methodology and state of the art of relevant topics. There is also a brief introduction of the historical material that will be processed in the later chapters, providing a clear motivation for the rest of the book and making the book as a whole more accessible to a technical audience. Meanwhile, a brief but solid preliminaries chapter brings a general (mathematically savvy) audience up to speed on the required technical background.

Chapters 3–6 address various specific topics: locating map elements, matching markers and labels, extracting building footprints, and georeferencing historical itineraries. Rather than summarizing the specific contributions – simply skip to page 6 for the introduction – I invite the reader to consider the broader picture that emerges from the book as a whole. Each time a specific task is considered, the author applies the *algorithmic lens*. (See the methodology section for a discussion of this concept.) In addition to providing interesting challenges for computer science, it brings a novel perspective to these tasks. This may be the most important conceptual contribution of the book: that it is possible – and indeed fruitful – to consider these kinds of challenges in the humanities from a computational perspective. A concept of particular importance turns out to be sensitivity analysis, and the reader would do well to include it in their toolbox: it is explicitly employed in Chapters 4 and 6, but is also recognizable in the uncertainty sampling of Chapter 3 and the Auto-ε algorithm of Chapter 5. Of course many of the other concepts applied in the book come recommended as well (such as Bayesian inference and graph algorithms), but none is as widely applied as this.

Finally, the conclusion provides a useful recap of the results from the previous chapters and includes an extensive per-chapter discussion of open problems and suggested future work. This is not to be misunderstood: rather than a list of shortcomings, it is a call to action based on positive experience. Indeed, the final paragraph argues that though not all problems are solved, the presented research program is fruitful and should be continued. I agree.

Dr. Thomas C. van Dijk
Chair for Computer Science
University of Würzburg

Contents

Chapter 1

Introduction

"A map does not just chart, it unlocks and formulates meaning; it forms bridges between here and there, between disparate ideas that we did not know were previously connected."

— Reif Larsen [Lar09]

Maps have always fascinated humans, and making maps is an integral part of human civilization. The earliest known maps are maps of the stars, there are cave paintings showing maps, and in antiquity, extensive Roman road maps. In the Middle Ages, *portolan* charts were made for the seafarers, and by the beginning of the early modern period sophisticated map projections emerged (for example due to Mercator). Later, methods for more accurate geodetic surveys were invented (for example by Gauß), leading eventually to the accurate and ubiquitous digital maps of our time. Of the multiplicity of maps created earlier in human history, it is safe to say that only a small fraction survived to the present day. An example of a map that has survived is presented in Figure 1.1: a clay tablet with a map of the ancient Babylonian city of Nippur, created approximately 3400 years ago. It is considered the earliest known map of a city. Artifacts like this are important pieces of our cultural heritage and must be preserved for future generations. What is more, their *contents* should be made accessible to the public in the most useful way.

Besides being valuable historical objects, historical maps are important sources of information for researchers in various scientific disciplines, especially in the humanities. This ranges from the actual history of cartography to general history as well as the geographic and social sciences. To give a nontrivial example: onomastics, the study of proper names, makes extensive use of historical maps.

Many libraries and archives have started digitizing their map collections. A basic level of digitization consists of scanned bitmap images, tagged with some basic bibliographic information such as title, author and year of production. However, in order to make the scanned maps searchable in more useful ways, a structured representation of the *contained information* is desirable. This includes information on the geographic features (such as labeled cities and rivers) and geopolitical features (such as political or administrative borders). We call information extraction at this level of semantic granularity *deep georeferencing* and will discuss it in more detail below. To get an impression of the wealth of information that can be contained in historical maps, see Figure 1.2.

Knowing about the features in a map enables queries that are useful for actual research practice, such as obtaining "all 17th century maps that include the surroundings of modern-day Würzburg," or comparing the evolution of place-name orthography in

Figure 1.1: Clay tablet showing a map of the Babylonian city of Nippur (approximately 1400 BC). It is considered the earliest city map still in existence and is currently preserved at the University of Jena.

different regions. It also enables the analysis of the geodetic accuracy or distortion of these maps, which is of historical and cartographic interest as well. In fact, being able to create a deep georeferencing for historical maps is a prerequisite for various applications. For example, Chiang [Chi15] recently expressed the need for a framework that would enable querying historical maps as a unified spatiotemporal data source, an effort that requires an in-depth extraction of information from historical maps. Also, rich data experiences such as New York Public Library's Space/Time Directory[1] and virtual reality applications [BGG⁺16] require detailed information on the content of maps. Ultimately, the information extracted from historical maps can become "a vital part of the larger data ecosystem" [Knu13].

Unfortunately, analyzing the contents of historical maps is a complex and time-consuming process. For the most part, this information extraction task is performed manually by experts – if at all. For example, it currently takes curators at the Würzburg University Library between 15 and 30 hours to georeference just the labeled settlements in a typical map from their *Franconica* collection.[2] To see why it takes so long, consider that the number of labeled place markers in a map can be in the order of several thousand.

Automated tools for extracting information from historical maps are scarce, for a variety of reasons. For one, there is a large variety of drawing styles in historical maps. This makes it hard for a single algorithm or software tool to automatically perform well on a large set of maps: look ahead at Figure 1.3 for some examples of the range of styles that occur within the *Franconica* collection. Secondly, there is the question of input. Historical maps can be quite inaccurate, deviate from modern cartographic conventions, or be in poor conservation state. When a historian georeferences a map, he or she brings a wealth of background information and the ability to do additional research when ambiguities

---

[1] http://spacetime.nypl.org/
[2] This collection contains approximately 800 maps created between the 16th and the 19th century, mainly covering the area of the historical Franconian Circle; see http://www.franconica-online.de/

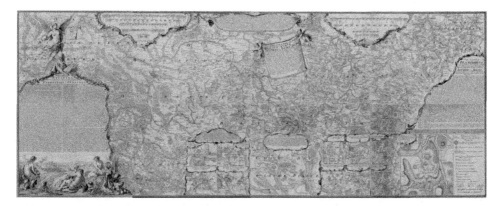

Figure 1.2: Isaak Jakob von Petri's *Chorographische Krieges-Carte von Zwickau bis Würtzburg*, published in 1759. It illustrates a military campaign of the Prussians during the Seven Years' War (1756–1763). The orientation of the map is not towards north, but follows the direction of the troop movements. Cartouches around the main map contain detailed textual descriptions of important battles, sketches of battle formations, and plans of the bivouacs marked with dates. The size of this map is 242×93 cm.

in the map require it. Finally, there is the issue of correctness: in general, algorithms for extracting semantic information from bitmap images are far from perfect. This is to be expected since these problems are truly difficult for computers. To the curators of historical map collections, however, the correctness of metadata can be of paramount importance (not to mention: a matter of pride).

1.1 Deep Georeferencing

The term *georeferencing* has different definitions in various research communities. For example, De By et al. [dBKS+01] define data to be georeferenced "if it is associated with some position using a spatial reference system." In their dictionary of geographic information systems [WS06], Wade and Sommer similarly define georeferencing as "aligning geographic data to a known coordinate system so it can be viewed, queried, and analyzed with other geographic data." Hackeloeer et al. [HKKM14] gives an overview over more definitions from various fields. Most of these definitions are based on the assumption that a meaningful transformation between the presentation of the geographic data and the target coordinate system exists, and that the challenge is to find this transformation. This assumption usually holds when dealing with modern maps or when working in a photogrammetric setting. However, it does not hold when dealing with historical maps: especially older maps are often heavily distorted and the cartographic techniques used to create them are unknown.

In addition, georeferencing in the above sense does not necessarily imply semantic meaning. Mapping pixels from a raster map to geo-coordinates complies perfectly with many common definitions of georeferencing. However, trying to answer the kind of queries discussed above, this information is not particularly useful, since it does not explicitly state *what* is actually on the map.[3]

We propose an extension to the concept of georeferencing to address these shortcomings in the domain of historical spatial data. We define *deep georeferencing* as linking spatial information contained in an unstructured document to spatial entities from a structured database. Note that this definition is not restricted to maps; it can be applied to any document containing spatial information.[4] Deep georeferencing is about linked data and semantics: spatial elements in a document are linked to known spatial entities, rather than to a coordinate system. The image and geographic coordinates are kept in this process, but the actual connection is made between entities, not coordinate systems. This is a fundamental difference to georeferencing in its common usage.[5]

Deep georeferencing relates to the research field of *geospatial semantics* (see Janowicz et al. [JSPH12] for an overview). Scheider et al. [SKO+11] propose a similar concept called *semantic referencing* in the context of modern maps and volunteered geographic information. A framework by Scheider and different group of co-authors [SJSK14] for encoding and querying the contents of historical maps can be used to store the information extracted by deep georeferencing. We note that while the idea of extracting semantic information from spatial documents is not entirely new, this is rarely done in practice when dealing with historical maps. Indeed, Southall [Sou13] observes that "the relatively limited use of historical maps within historical GIS [...] is due in large part to the enormous amount of work required to convert from digital images of maps, even geo-referenced map images, to [...] representations of the *features* on the maps."

Consider the Babylonian city map from Figure 1.1. It has been studied extensively by multiple scientists. Every single stroke in the carving has been analyzed and the depicted details have largely been identified. This includes references to known historical entities (such as, for example, temples that are known to have existed in Nippur), but also to the remains at the present-day archaeological excavation site [Kra81]. The information resulting from this research, in its semantics and granularity, can be considered excellent deep georeferencing. The extensive manual efforts involved in the deep georeferencing of this artifact were most likely spent because of its singular historical importance. It is unfortunate that for the vast majority of historical maps no such information is available.

There exist some tools that help with extracting information from historical maps, for example by providing convenient graphical user interfaces; a detailed discussion of related software systems follows in Chapter 2. We will see that there are only few tools that actually *automate* steps in the process of deeply georeferencing historical maps. In this book, we tackle this lack of automation and propose several systems that combine

---

[3] Consider for example searching for maps showing a certain small village. Its geo-location is obviously covered by any world map, but the village is probably marked in none. Based on coordinates alone, it is impossible to answer this type of query in a satisfying way when dealing with a wide variety of maps.

[4] Such documents include for example historical itineraries, which we will consider in Chapter 6.

[5] We use the term "georeferencing" many times throughout this book, and we mean deep georeferencing unless otherwise noted.

efficient algorithms with smart user interactions to make information extraction from historical maps more efficient.

1.2 Methodology

We cannot expect a computer to fully automatically extract all information contained in a historical map, since this involves semantics and is therefore truly hard: it is about *understanding* unstructured data, which in general still requires human intelligence. On the other hand, we cannot expect humans to manually process historical maps without help, because there are simply too many of these maps and there is too much information on them. The methodology used in this book combines the strengths of both computers and humans: we devise efficient algorithms to largely automate information extraction tasks and pair these algorithms with smart user interactions to handle what is not understood by the algorithm.

The Algorithmic Lens. Throughout this book, we approach problems by applying the *algorithmic lens*. This is a methodology in which we view complex systems "in terms of their computational requirements and the way they transform information." This "allows us to apply the concepts of computer science [...] giving new insights and new ways of thinking" [Kar11].

In the context of the present book, this means that we analyze problems that have their origin in the humanities from a computer science perspective. We start by splitting large, underspecified tasks (like: understand this map) into smaller pieces in order to get manageable problems. This modular approach allows for rigorous problem statements and, thereby, reproducible experiments and comparability; this is in contrast to monolithic software systems, where it can be unclear how any specific detail influences the outcome. Competing systems for a certain step can then be proposed and evaluated. Such a "separation of concerns" in systems for processing historical maps is also advocated, for example, by Shaw and Bajcsy [SB11] and Schöneberg et al. [SSH13].

When splitting information extraction problems into smaller parts, we try to follow the process a human (reading a map) would apply: first finding an element of interest on the map, then reading its corresponding label, and then relating this information to, for example, a modern map. Following this "human" approach makes it easier to design semantically meaningful sub-problems and appropriate user interactions.

Working on these problems, we make sure to understand each problem in the context of its own domain (the humanities). Based on this understanding, we properly model the problem as a computer scientist and algorithm designer. In particular, we do not think of computer science as an auxiliary science and do not simply apply basic techniques as black boxes: the modeling step rewards computer-science creativity and is the core of our contributions in this book. Based on a formal model, we devise algorithms to solve the problem optimally and efficiently.

Smart User Interaction. Besides producing a solution, a proper modeling of the problems also allows us to derive additional information. An example of this is *sensitivity analysis*, which we apply to various problems throughout this book. Sensitivity analysis can be used to power smart user interactions, for example by identifying parts of a solution that might require manual verification. In this way, users do not have to carefully inspect all of the solution, but are efficiently guided to the parts that actually *need* their attention. Sensitivity analysis can also provide information on the quality of alternate solutions. Sometimes, parts of these solutions are actually correct and can be presented to a user as possible alternatives. Ideally, we can guide the user to problematic parts of the automatic solution and simultaneously present meaningful alternatives.

In addition to sensitivity analyses (which are mainly suitable for post-processing) we also apply *crowdsourcing*. Crowdsourcing is a technique in which (small) problems are solved by a crowd of volunteers, typically working via an online platform. For quality assurance, the same tasks are usually solved independently by several users.

Successfully applying crowdsourcing to a given problem can be challenging. First, since the users are usually laypeople, the crowdsourcing tasks have to be designed well: they need to be easily understood and correctly solvable without background knowledge. Second, appropriate algorithms are needed to integrate the different user answers. In this book, we particularly focus on the second challenge. We show that carefully designed algorithms enable offering attractive user interfaces to the crowd (which is crucial for the success of a crowdsourcing project), while still being able to efficiently handle the crowd's answers.

1.3   Outline of this Book

This book is organized as follows. Our main contributions are presented in Chapters 3 through 6. Chapters 3 and 4 deal with problems occurring on medium-scale maps from the early modern period. Chapter 5 focuses on more recent, large-scale city atlases, and Chapter 6 deals with a textual representation of spatial data in the form of historical itineraries. For a detailed discussion of the individual types of documents, together with other preliminaries, see Chapter 2.

Locating Map Elements. First, we focus on the arguably most fundamental problem of our information extraction task: *finding* specific elements in historical maps. Relevant elements can be pictograms (for instance: place markers), but can also include individual characters from text labels. Knowing about the occurrence and location of such elements in a map is essential for any subsequent information extraction step.

The main challenge in this task is caused by the considerable visual variations in the drawing of the individual elements. See Figure 1.3 for examples of pictograms and text from four different historical maps. These maps belong to the same map collection, show parts of the same region, and have been created within a timespan of 150 years. Still, the visual style of the contained elements varies strongly across the different maps. There is

Figure 1.3: Place markers and text on several historical maps from the Franconica collection, created between 1533 and 1676. Note the variety of visual styles, both in the pictographs and the lettering.

even a significant variance *within* a single map: consider for example the 🏰 pictograms in the left-most map, which share a similar shape, but each feature individual details.

In Chapter 3, we approach this problem by applying *template matching*, which is a standard technique from image processing. It takes a template (manually selected for the specific map) and finds a set of candidate matches on the map. Because of the variations in drawing, this set is likely to contain false positives and the problem remains to determine which of these matches are in fact semantically correct. This (semantic) problem cannot be expected to be solved automatically. Instead, we present an active learning system that makes efficient use of a user's manual effort in order to reliably distinguish between correct and incorrect matches. Using the *uncertainty sampling* strategy [SU07], our approach iteratively presents batches of matches to the user. These are carefully selected so that the user's time and effort is spent where it is most useful.

Our approach works for various template matching algorithms and can easily be transfered to other domains: we also apply it to a related problem, the detection of certain glyphs in books printed in the early modern period (so-called *incunables*). We present user interfaces and an open-source software package implementing our approach. Finally, we show that our approach (and our software) work well in practice, both experimentally and by a user study.

Matching Markers and Labels. Elements on historical maps are often densely packed. This can make it particularly challenging to find out which text label corresponds to the various markers. Figure 1.4 shows two examples: in the situation on the left, map elements are arranged very densely, which demands some combinatorial reasoning by the reader to figure out the correct correspondence between markers and labels. The situation on the right is different in the sense that based on the map alone, it is not possible at all to determine the correct correspondence. (Look ahead to Figure 4.12 on page 70 for more details on this situation.) Still, in most situations, labels are at least placed *near* the object they refer to.

In Chapter 4, we use this simple observation to model an optimization problem based on bipartite matchings. We present an efficient algorithm for the problem and show experimentally that it is able to match markers and corresponding labels with high accu-

Figure 1.4: Historical map with densely arranged map elements (left) and ambiguous label placement (right). In both situations, it is difficult to identify which label belongs to which place marker.

racy. In particular, complicated situations like the one shown in Figure 1.4 (left) can be solved automatically using our approach. For the situation shown on the right, things are different: since the placement of the labels is ambiguous, we cannot find the correct assignment without external help. Again, we introduce an efficient user interaction that effectively leads the user to such unclear situations, and present a prototype interface.

Our approach requires the correct extent and location of each marker and label as its input. However, this information might not always be available in practice, for example due to errors in a previous recognition step. We extend our approach to a problem formulation that allows labels to be split, which is a reasonable error to expect. Unfortunately, this version of the problem is NP-hard. For a restricted version of this problem, we present a polynomial-time algorithm.

Extracting Building Footprints. Large-scale maps provide different challenges than the medium-scale maps discussed before do. The higher level of detail makes it possible to extract not only the position, but also the *shape* of objects. Objects of interest include for example building footprints, streets, and bodies of water. The New York Public Library (NYPL) has been working on the extraction of building footprints from 19th-century insurance atlases for some years. They use *crowdsourcing* to cope with this extraction task on their extensive collection of maps. This means that the steps involving user interaction are dealt with by volunteers using an online platform[6]. See Figure 1.5 for an example of their large-scale maps (showing building footprints in Manhattan), together with a crowdsourcing user interface.

The NYPL applies a three-stage extraction process, starting with an automatic detection of footprints using image processing techniques. This first step does not involve human supervision, but often leads to incorrect (or imprecise) recognition results. In the second step, the automatically detected footprints are presented to users for manual verification. Users can declare footprints as "correct", "incorrect" or "to be fixed" (when the recognition result is imprecise, but not entirely wrong). The footprint polygons from the last category are addressed in the third step, which again involves user interaction.

---

[6] http://buildinginspector.nypl.org/

Figure 1.5: Section from a New York insurance atlas, showing building footprints in Manhattan in 1894. A user is tracing one of the footprints (dashed red line) using the NYPL's crowdsourcing interface: vertices can manually be added, deleted or moved (by dragging the red drops).

These polygons are presented with an interface that allows users to add, delete, and move vertices in order to make the polygon match the underlying building footprint (see again Figure 1.5).

For quality assurance, the same tasks are solved by several users independently. This raises questions on how to integrate the user-submitted data, particularly for the third step: how to find the consensus for a set of (possibly different) polygons that are supposed to trace the same building footprint?

In Chapter 5, we formalize the process currently used in the crowdsourcing system and give an algorithm for calculating consensus polygons. Using an extensive data set collected by the NYPL, we experimentally evaluate our algorithm and show that it significantly improves the quality of the resulting data (as compared to the individual user-submitted polygons). In addition, we discuss a variant of our algorithm that is parameter-free. Note that in this chapter, we approach efficient user interaction from a slightly different perspective than in the previous two: rather than minimizing the work required of the individual users, we effectively *combine* the users' efforts to achieve a result quality higher than that of any individual user.

Georeferencing Itineraries.   Finally, we consider historical itineraries, which provide quite a different representation of spatial information. Unlike the geometric representation of the (more or less complete) geography of a region provided by maps, itineraries contain a *textual* representation focused on individual travel routes. They describe these routes as a sequence of settlements encountered along the way, together with the travel distances between them. Sometimes, this description is augmented with additional information on the settlements, for instance a categorization based on size or town privileges. The information contained in these documents is of interest to several disciplines in the humanities and relevant for various research topics, including the investigation of early modern period road networks and the development of human mobility. Figure 1.6 (left) shows an itinerary from a historical guidebook published in the 16th century. It describes the route from Salzburg to Innsbruck, including seven settlements along the way.

Georeferencing these documents, that is, identifying each historical settlement on a modern map, provides several challenges. First, many toponyms have changed sig-

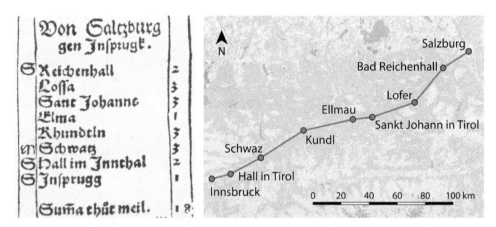

Figure 1.6: *Left:* itinerary from the *Raißbüchlin*, a guidebook published in 1563, describing the route from Salzburg to Innsbruck. *Right:* the same route on a modern map, showing corresponding modern places.

nificantly over time, particularly in terms of their spelling. The itinerary from Figure 1.6 shows for example two different spellings for the place "Innsbruck" (within a single page), none of which match its modern spelling. However, many toponyms (and their modern spellings) have remained *phonetically* similar. Second, the distances given in the itineraries are imprecise: they are often rounded to integers, the road network they refer to is unknown, and the way the distances were measured is also unclear. Despite all these uncertainties, historical itineraries clearly contain valuable information that can be used to reconstruct the described routes.

In Chapter 6, we introduce a probabilistic approach that calculates a most-likely assignment of the places given in a historical itinerary to modern map data. It is able to deal with the discussed uncertainties, including assessing whether the difference between two toponym strings is a phonetically plausible change. Our experimental evaluation shows that our approach achieves high accuracy on itineraries from historical guidebooks. In addition, we show that sensitivity analysis can be used as the basis for an efficient quality assurance process, in which our algorithm selects uncertain assignments for manual user verification.

Chapter 2

Preliminaries

In this chapter, we give a short historical overview over each type of spatial document we will consider in this book. Furthermore, we review related work that is relevant to the topic of information extraction from historical maps in general. (Related work that is specific to the individual topics of the following chapters is discussed there.) In the final section of this chapter, we introduce basic definitions and present methods that are used throughout the remainder of the book.

2.1 Historical Spatial Documents

In the subsequent chapters of this book, we deal with three different types of historical documents providing spatial information: medium-scale maps, large-scale insurance atlases, and itineraries. We give a short introduction to the origins and specific characteristics of each of these document types below.

Medium-Scale Maps. Chapter 3 and 4 deal with information extraction from historical maps of medium scale. We particularly focus on maps created between the 16th and 18th century, thus spanning the time from the High Renaissance to the end of the Age of Enlightenment. Our main source for maps is the *Franconica* collection[1] maintained by the Würzburg University Library. This collection contains approximately 800 maps with a focus on Franconia from that timespan. Part of the collection is the famous *Rotenhan* map from 1533 (see Figure 2.1a), which is considered to be the first map of Franconia [Meu07]. We have selected this set of maps because of its wide production timespan over three centuries, its visual and technical variety, and its broad range of (medium) scales: in our experiments, we worked with maps of scales between approximately 1:300 000 and 1:700 000. Of course, there are many more (and also much larger) collections of historical maps. For example, the map collection of the Bavarian State Library contains 80 000 maps created before 1850, and the IKAR database[2] lists 260 000 of such maps. Outside of Germany, the British Library and the Library of Congress both have extensive map collections, each holding more than 4.5 million maps.

Historical maps from the time between the 16th and 18th century are very diverse in size, make, purpose, and style. In his introduction to cartography in the German lands, Meurer [Meu07] describes Renaissance cartography as "a mosaic of individual

---

[1] http://www.franconica-online.de/
[2] http://ikar.staatsbibliothek-berlin.de/

parts differing in type and importance." This diversity is due to several factors. First, cartography at that time was not a well-established discipline, and lacked common rules and standards.[3] Instead, a variety of different map styles, often based on medieval or ancient model, continued to coexist. Second, different techniques were applied to produce maps. At the beginning of the Renaissance, woodcutting was the predominant technique for printing maps. In the middle of the 16th century, copper engraving gained increasing popularity as a map production method, but woodcutting was still being used until the 17th century [Meu07]. Using either technique, it was difficult to accurately engrave small text [Woo07b]. This led not only to variety between several maps, but also to considerable variance between the individual characters within a *single* map. Third, the political and territorial fragmentation of Germany was "reflected in a large number of regional maps, [whose] quality and function differ enormously" [Meu07].

In general, geodetic accuracy was low. On maps created before the late 18th century, coordinates and projection grids were sometimes present, but "the data behind them was often questionable" [Woo07a]. At the time, the interest in surveying was still mostly qualitative: instead of providing geodetic accuracy, "maps relied on extensive labeling of place-names" [Woo07b] to convey geographic information. This was not only due to difficulties in surveying and map production, but also because of the (technical) inability of map *users* to accurately determine the geographic coordinates of their own current position.

Despite this lack of geodetic accuracy, maps from that time offer a wealth of information. Many maps include large numbers of labeled place markers that are densely packed and use different pictograms indicating various types of settlements. On a larger scale, territories are often indicated by the background color of the corresponding map area. In terms of physical geography, one typically sees waters, woodlands, and hills. While river systems are depicted in high detail (including smaller tributaries), on many maps there is a striking absence of a road network.[4] Forests and hills are indicated only qualitatively by an accumulation of pictograms. For examples of all these features, see Figure 2.1.

In the context of information extraction and georeferencing, both the visual diversity and geographic inaccuracy of historical maps pose considerable challenges. For one, the individual characteristics make it difficult to develop methods that work well on a variety of different historical maps. When developing the approaches presented in Chapter 3 and 4, we put special emphasis on robustness against such differences and ran experiments on maps from different centuries. In addition, there are inconsistencies within a single map, like place markers that are missing text labels and vice versa. (For examples of this occurring in several maps, look ahead at Figure 4.4.) The typically dense labeling, together with small, hand-engraved text, can make it challenging to read labels and

---

[3] There was, for example, no agreement on the orientation of maps. Although relatively small, the Franconica collection contains maps that are oriented towards north, east, and south. This is not necessarily indicated on the map.

[4] Some exceptions to this exist, a prominent example being Erhard Etzlaub's *Rom Weg* map from 1500. This map was intended for pilgrims and shows roads from central Europe towards Rome [Meu07].

(a) Section of Sebastian von Rotenhan: *Das Franckenlandt*, 1533.

(b) Section of Frederik De Wit: *Circulus Franconicus*, 1706.

(c) Section of Johann Baptist Homann: *Erster und gröster Theil des [...] Franckischen Craisses*, 1710.

(d) Section of Daniel Adam Hauer: *Carte Topographique D'Allemagne*, 1787.

Figure 2.1: Sections of historical maps from *Franconica* collection, containing a variety of information, including rivers, woodlands, hills, political borders, and (labeled) settlements.

find their corresponding markers. Finally, the lack of geographic accuracy prevents a straight-forward alignment of the historical map to modern map data.

Historical maps usually contain additional information arranged around the actual map body, such as legends, city views, extensive titles, and instructions to the reader. While we acknowledge that this information is interesting and certainly worth analyzing, extracting it is beyond the scope of this book. The main reasons are that the additional information is mostly not spatial, presented in an unstructured way, and (at least in the case of titles) often already extracted by hand during digitization.

Large-Scale Insurance Atlases.　In Chapter 5, we are concerned with information extraction from more recent, large-scale maps. In cooperation with the New York Public Library (NYPL), we considered a set of 12 fire insurance atlases, containing nearly 600 individual map sheets in total. The NYPL has been actively working on digitizing their collection of insurance atlases for several years using various approaches [Knu13]. The specific set of 12 atlases that we experimented with is the current corpus for their *Building Inspector*[5] crowdsourcing website. On this website, volunteers can help extract building footprints and transcribe the corresponding labels from these maps. The atlases were published between 1855 and 1915 and cover several boroughs of New York City. The contained map sheets are of scale 1:600 (one inch to 50 feet), which was the standard scale of North American fire insurance atlases.

For a history of fire insurance mapping, see the introduction by Ristow [Ris68]. He notes that fire insurance maps presumably originated in the late 18th century, when the first fire insurance map of London was published. Some 50 years later, in the mid-19th century, fire insurance maps became popular with North American insurance companies. For the growing fire insurance industry, it was no longer economic to inspect each building to be insured on-site. This fueled a demand for insurance maps, which provided quickly accessible, accurate information on fire risks on a per-building level. By the beginning of the 20th century, the *Sanborn Map Company* had absorbed most of its competitors and established a de-facto monopoly on fire insurance maps in the United States. In the following 30 years, Sanborn insurance maps were in widespread use, until they were gradually replaced by other technology in the 1940s. The surviving copies of these maps are now considered "invaluable [...] records of America's urban development" [Ris68] over a timespan of 100 years.

The spatial and technical information provided in fire insurance maps was surveyed specifically for making these maps by teams of surveyors. The individual map sheets were hand-drawn and reproduced using lithography; the color was applied afterwards using watercolor tint. Often, the map sheets were subsequently bound to large volumes covering specific areas. In order to account for recent changes (for example when a building was demolished and replaced), Sanborn offered a correction service that supplied paper patches showing the updated situation for pasting into the maps.

---

[5] http://buildinginspector.nypl.org/

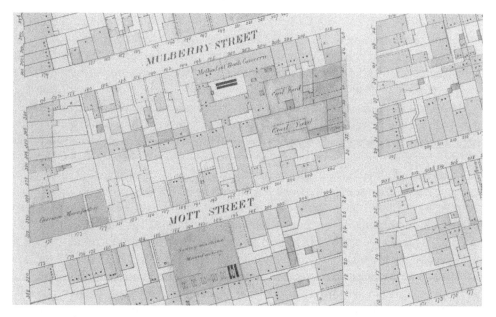

Figure 2.2: Section of a fire insurance map showing blocks in Lower Manhattan. This map sheet is taken from William Perris' *Maps of the City of New York*, an insurance atlas published between 1857 and 1862. Perris' mapping business was later acquired by the *Sanborn Map Company*. Note the use of various colors and symbols (such as open and closed circles), which provide information on the construction type and individual fire hazard for each building.

Insurance atlases usually contain a collection of map sheets covering specific neighborhoods of a city. Due to their large scale, the map sheets present streets and building footprints in considerable detail. Typically, each footprint has a colored background, which indicates the construction material and build style of the corresponding building. In addition, symbols (such as circles or crosses) give additional information on possible fire hazards. On the example map presented in Figure 2.2, footprints colored green indicate a particular fire hazard. They are further subdivided according to comparative danger as indicated by the number of symbols inside, ranging from one (for example a bakery) to four (for example firework manufactories).

In addition to information on buildings, insurance maps also provide street names and street numbers for easier orientation. In our work, we are mainly interested in extracting the polygonal shapes of building footprints. The NYPL currently asks crowd-sourcing users to manually extract street names and numbers; however, the consistent handwriting might facilitate automatic approaches as well.

Itineraries. In Chapter 6, we deal with historical spatial documents that are quite different from the various maps we have discussed above: historical itineraries. Itineraries describe a route by listing the settlements encountered along the way and indicating the travel distances between those settlements. Interestingly, they were a much more common tool for wayfinding than maps in the Renaissance, since many maps lacked road networks altogether. As such, itineraries "were by no means replaced by their graphic equivalents" [Woo07a]. Instead, historical itineraries coexist with maps and sometimes even served as data sources for compiling maps [Meu07].

Historical itineraries were usually part of roadbooks, which were printed in small formats so they could be carried while traveling. A large number of these books are still in existence today: for example, the Austrian National Library owns approximately 50 books of itineraries published between 1500 and 1800, with an additional 400 at SUB Göttingen, and 75 at HAB Wolfenbüttel. In the present book, we consider two historical guidebooks from the late-16th century, each containing hundreds of itineraries: Jörg Gail's *Raißbüchlin* [Krü74], published in Augsburg in 1563 as the first independently printed German guidebook, and *Kronn und Auszbunde aller Wegweiser* [Ano97], published anonymously in Köln in 1597. Figure 2.3 shows a page from each book. For an introduction to historical guidebooks (and specifically the *Raißbüchlin*), see Krüger [Krü74].

The two guidebooks we consider in this book were printed using movable type and are both set in a tabular form, listing names of encountered places together with the travel distance from the previous place. Both books give the sum of the distance of the individual legs, thus providing the total travel distance for each itinerary. In addition, there are indicators for the importance of each place, based on the respective town privileges. For example, the *Raißbüchlin* prepends "S", "M", "D", and "K" to some toponyms, indicating that these places are cities, market towns, villages, or monasteries.

Despite the similarities and the relatively small timespan between their publication, the two guidebooks are quite different in terms of their organization and layout. The *Raißbüchlin* is rather minimalistic, starting with a short introduction and then simply giving a sequence of itineraries. The page layout is plain and focuses on one route at a time. In contrast, the itineraries in the *Kronn und Auszbunde aller Wegweiser* are grouped by city of departure and then ordered alphabetically. This roadbook uses a three-column layout and has maps enclosed with it, which provide an overview of the covered areas and are referred to from each itinerary. In addition, there is a short description of each city of departure.

Identifying the places from historical itineraries can be challenging. The toponyms given in our two roadbooks from the late-16th century have usually changed by now, at least in their spelling. This makes it difficult to find the corresponding modern toponyms (for instance in a gazetteer[6]). Consider for example the first stop in the itinerary from Augsburg to Salzburg given in Figure 2.3 (left): it is spelled "Mitelsteten", but it has also been mentioned under the names of "Mütelsteten", "Mittelsteten", "Mittelnsteten", "Myttelstetten", "Müttelstetten", and "Mittelstätten" between the 14th century and now [FvR13]. Nowadays, the name of the village is spelled "Mittelstetten." All the historical spellings are at least phonetically similar to the modern one, so that a researcher would be able

---

[6] A gazetteer is a dictionary of place names, sometimes also including geo-coordinates and additional information on the places.

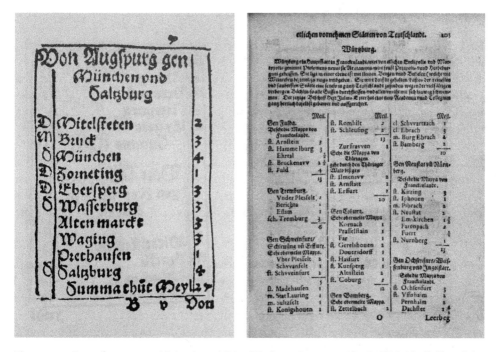

Figure 2.3: Pages from two guidebooks published in the 16th century, the *Raißbüchlin* (left) and the *Kronn und Auszbunde aller Wegweiser* (right).

to manually figure out the relation. However, this is not the case for all toponyms. In Chapter 6, we will for example encounter a place in the *Raißbüchlin* called "Jesta", which is now called "Oestheim." Without the (geographic) context provided by the itinerary, it would have been very difficult to make this relation.[7]

Digitization. Digitizing historical documents, in the sense of transferring a physical artifact into the digital world, is a difficult task. It requires profound knowledge about the documents as not to damage them during the process and also sophisticated technical equipment (usually based on scanning or photography). In addition, digitization demands some farsightedness when defining long-term storage formats – and not to mention a good lot of patience. The process of creating high-quality digital representations from raw material is beyond the scope of the present book. Rather, we assume that this work has already be done before, and when we refer to maps (or other historical documents) in this book, we mean *digital images* of them. For more information on the topic, refer to Jobst's overview book [Job10].

---

[7] In fact, there is a guidebook from the mid-16th century that lists this village as "Ehsta" and explicitly mentions that in many other guidebooks, the village is called "Jesta."

2.2 Related Software Systems

Since the digitization and analysis of historical maps is of increasing interest to libraries and archives, several systems simplifying this complex process have been developed. These systems can be divided into two categories. First, there are systems that are generally suitable for georeferencing elements in any historical map. Most of these systems provide convenient graphical interfaces, but still rely heavily on users to manually annotate or georeference the input maps. Second, there are systems that focus on extracting particular details from a particular set of maps. These approaches are usually specifically tailored to a large corpus of maps containing hundreds or thousands of map sheets that have been created with the same methods in a coherent visual style. As a result, these systems cannot be easily transfered to other maps (of a different style). They are often aimed at experts, do not provide user interfaces, and have only proof-of-concept implementations.

General Purpose Systems. The *Pelagios* project[8] by Simon et al. [SBI12] provides tools for creating linked open data describing historical places. This task is not limited to maps, but also includes places mentioned in text as well as shown in arbitrary images. Part of this project is the *Recogito* georeferencing system [SBIdSC15]. This software is provided as a web service and features a convenient user interface for annotating spatial elements in text and images. However, the system does not provide a significant level of automation, especially when working with maps: in the current version, users have to locate and annotate map labels manually. Simon et al. [SPIB14] describe preliminary work on automating these tasks, but this has never been implemented in the production system. Since the *Pelagios* project has pledged itself to open source and the *Recogito* system is modularly structured, it may be possible to integrate some of the approaches described in the present book into this system.

With a different group of co-authors, Simon [SHRM11] introduced the *YUMA* map annotation tool, which was later used as a base for the *Maphub* platform[9] by Haslhofer et al. [HRLG13]. Both systems support manual annotation of historical maps, but do not offer tools to automatically extract information from the maps. The development of this software has been discontinued as of 2013.

Fleet et al. [FKP12] present the *Georeferencer* system[10], which is part of a commercial toolbox offered by *Klokan Technologies*. The system supports *georectifying* historical maps, which means transforming them into a known coordinate system based on manually selected control points. Note that this does not qualify as deep georeferencing, since usually only few map elements are referenced to their modern counterparts and no semantic information is stored. Still, georectifying maps enables spatial query interfaces such as *OldMapsOnline*[11] [SP12]. This web service shows historical maps embedded into

---

[8] http://commons.pelagios.org/
[9] http://maphub.github.io/
[10] http://www.georeferencer.com/
[11] http://www.oldmapsonline.org/

a modern overview map; when zooming or panning the modern map, historical maps covering a similar area are presented.

To semi-automatically detect and georeference places, Höhn et al. [HSS13] propose a system that finds place markers based on examples a user has previously identified. In a subsequent step, this system suggests possible place names using a modern map. Work on this system has recently been resumed by Höhn and Schommer [HS17b], but no comprehensive description or implementation has been published yet. In another paper, Höhn and Schommer [HS17a] propose georeferencing the contents of a historical map in relation to another historical map (as opposed to a modern map). This is a promising approach since it was not unusual for historical maps to be "pirated and roughly copied" [Woo07a] in order to create new maps. In such cases, two historical maps may be much more similar to each other than to a modern map. Provided that one of these maps has already been georeferenced, it is possible to use this information to georeference to other historical map as well.

For the postprocessing of georectified maps, Jenny and Hurni [JH11] introduce *Map-Analyst*, a tool that is able to analyze the geometric and geodetic accuracy of historical maps and visualize the identified distortions. The underlying method requires a sufficient number of control points between the historical and the modern map as its input.

Systems for Particular Corpora. Research on fully-automatic information retrieval specifically from historical maps is scarce. Automatic approaches exist, but only for restricted inputs – that is, developed specifically to digitize a particular corpus.

For example, a topic that is actively being worked on is the automatic extraction of forest cover from historical maps. Leyk et al. [LBW06, LB09] describe methods to find forest cover in a specific set of 19th-century topographic maps (the so-called *Siegfried Atlas*). Ostafin et al. [OIK+17] pursue the same objective on several sets of early-20th century maps. Their approach mainly relies on color segmentation and the authors find that it has difficulties when the original colors have degraded, which is frequently the case in older maps. Kaim et al. [KKK+16] introduce another method for extracting forest cover from historical maps and apply it successfully to two corpora from the late-19th and early-20th century. The authors conclude that their approach might be applicable to other maps from the 19th century as well. Iosifescu et al. [ITH16] describe a workflow for vectorizing features from the *Siegfried Atlas* using existing software tools. Their method is not limited to extracting forest cover, but relies on several parameters that need to be manually picked for each kind of feature to be extracted.

In cooperation with the Saxon State and University Library Dresden (SLUB), Bill et al. [BWM14] present a method to automatically analyze map sheets from a specific corpus, the so-called *Messtischblätter*.[12] This is a set of maps created between 1870 and 1943, providing high geographic accuracy as well as a consistent visual style. In particular, the cartographic projection and the coordinates of the four corners of each map sheet are known. The authors focus on detecting those four corners (of the map body), which

---

[12] http://www.deutschefotothek.de/cms/kartenforum-sachsen-messtischblaetter.xml

allows them to separate the map from the border of the sheet. This enables a seamless presentation of several map sheets together and a precise projection to other coordinate systems. In a second study, Bill et al. [BKW15] compare the accuracy when solving this problem either by using image processing or instead by applying a crowdsourcing approach. The authors conclude that the two approaches lead to a similar accuracy. Note that the extracted information does not qualify for deep georeferencing: Bill et al.'s process aligns coordinate systems, but does not consider the actual contents of the maps.

Giraldo Arteaga [GA13] automatically extracts building footprints from georectified scans of the fire insurance atlases discussed in Section 2.1. In a subsequent step, the extraction results are manually checked by volunteers. We discuss this crowdsourcing process in more detail in Chapter 5.

Chiang and Knoblock [CK13b] introduce a method for extracting road networks from printed maps and implemented it as part of their *Strabo* map processing framework. Their system achieves high accuracy while requiring only limited user effort. However, it is focused on maps meeting 20th-century cartographic standards, which is not the case with older historical maps.

The effectiveness of the approaches discussed above is in part due to the homogeneity of the relatively recent maps they are developed for. Note that the experiments in Chapter 3 and 4 are performed on more diverse and much older maps (16th to 18th century, see Section 2.1).

Optical Character Recognition. Optical character recognition (OCR) is the problem of recognizing text in raster images and transforming it to machine-readable text. Since historical maps are digitized as raster images and usually contain a large number of text labels, OCR is relevant to many information extraction tasks on these documents. Several general-purpose OCR systems are available as integrated software packages. This includes commercial software like *FineReader*[13] as well as open-source tools like *Tesseract*[14] [Smi07]. Recently, OCR systems based on deep learning techniques have emerged, of which the *OCRopus* system[15] by Breuel et al. [Bre08, BUHAAS13] is a popular example. Note that the latter is not an integrated system but rather a toolkit aimed at experts.

General-purpose OCR systems are often aimed at modern, typewritten texts and do not perform well on historical maps due to lower printing quality and higher visual variation. However, many systems can be manually trained to handle uncommon scripts or fonts by providing explicit training material. Such an approach can work well – Kirchner et al. [KDBN16] reach high accuracy with *Tesseract* even on early prints from the 15th century – but preparing the training data is nontrivial and requires significant manual effort. Specific training is therefore only reasonable when dealing with a large corpus of text that uses a consistent script or font.

There are some OCR approaches that are designed specifically for extracting text from (historical) maps. Chiang and Knoblock [CK15] present an approach to extract

---

[13] https://www.abbyy.com/finereader
[14] https://github.com/tesseract-ocr/tesseract
[15] https://github.com/tmbdev/ocropy

text layers from raster maps. They use their method to first locate the text labels and subsequently pass them (individually) to the commercial *FineReader* OCR system. The authors show that by applying their segmentation as a preprocessing step, they clearly outperform running *FineReader* directly on the entire map image. While originally only tested on modern maps, Chiang et al. [CLHN+16] and Yu et al. [YLC16] extend this approach to historical maps from the 19th and 20th century.

Höhn [Höh17] proposes an OCR system for historical maps based on deep learning. The system is specifically aimed at recognizing text labels on maps and achieves high accuracy in preliminary tests on *portolan charts* from the early modern period. While this approach is promising, it seems to require an extensive amount of training data and is not published in full detail yet.

Weinman [Wei13] pursues a different direction and additionally takes a gazetteer into account. He introduces a probabilistic approach that matches gazetteer entries with toponyms from the map that have been previously identified using a system for scene text recognition [WBKF14]. Limiting the possible recognition results to the set of strings contained in the gazetteer makes this approach more robust against possible recognition errors. In addition, Weinman's method takes the spatial relation between the location of the toponyms on the map and the geo-location of the corresponding places from the gazetteer into account.

While we acknowledge the relevance of OCR to information extraction from historical maps, we do not address the problem of OCR in this book. There are several promising developments on OCR for historical maps, but at this point, the problem must still be considered open. We make some proposals on this topic in the concluding Chapter 7.

2.3 Algorithmic Foundations

In this section, we introduce basic definitions and notation used throughout this book. Furthermore, we discuss some of the algorithmic techniques used in the following chapters. We point to Cormen et al. [CLRS09] for a standard reference book on algorithms. Our notation largely follows the definitions from this book. See Shalev-Shwartz and Ben-David [SSBD14] for a more extensive background on machine learning and Russel and Norvig [RN09] for an introduction to probabilistic reasoning.

2.3.1 Graphs, Matchings, and Flows

A *graph* is a tuple $G = (V, E)$, consisting of a set of *vertices* V and a set of *edges* E. Vertices are also referred to as *nodes*; we use both terms synonymously. In an *undirected graph*, an edge is an unordered pair $\{u, v\}$ of vertices $u, v \in V$. Following common convention, we denote edges of undirected graphs as (u, v) for the remainder of this book (identifying (u, v) and (v, u)). In a *directed graph*, an edge is an ordered pair (u, v) and also called *arc*. In both directed and undirected graphs, we forbid *self-loops*, that is, edges (u, v) with $u = v$. If not explicitly specified, we assume graphs to be undirected.

In a graph $G = (V, E)$, two vertices $u, v \in V$ are called *adjacent* if there exists an edge $(u, v) \in E$. An edge $(u, v) \in E$ is called *incident* to u and v; u and v are called *incident* to (u, v). A *path* in a directed graph is a sequence of vertices such that there exists an arc in E for each pair of consecutive vertices. A path is called *simple* if it does not contain any vertex more than once. If a path begins and ends at the same vertex (and contains more than one vertex), we say the path forms a *cycle*. If a directed graph contains no cycles, it is called a directed *acyclic* graph. A cycle in which all vertices except the first and the last are pairwise different is called a *simple* cycle. For the remainder of this book, we assume paths and cycles to be simple, unless otherwise noted.

Matchings. Given an undirected graph, a subset $M \subseteq E$ is called a *matching* if each vertex in V is incident to at most one edge in M. A matching is called *maximum* if it is of maximum cardinality, that is, if there exists no matching M' with $|M'| > |M|$. If a matching has size $|V|/2$, that is, if all vertices in G are incident to an edge in M, the matching is called *perfect*.

Finding a maximum matching in a given graph is a classic problem in combinatorics. A polynomial-time algorithm for this problem on general graphs is due to Edmonds [Edm65]; it runs in $O(V^2 E)$ time. The problem can also be expressed using integer linear programming as follows. For each edge $e \in E$, let x_e be a binary variable that indicates whether e is part of the matching or not. To obtain a maximum matching, maximize the sum of all x_e under the constraint that no vertex is incident to more than one edge in the matching:

$$\text{maximize} \quad \sum_{e \in E} x_e \tag{2.1}$$

$$\text{subject to} \quad \sum_{v \in V} x_{(u,v)} \leq 1 \quad \forall u \in V \tag{2.2}$$

$$x_e \in \{0, 1\} \quad \forall e \in E. \tag{2.3}$$

An undirected graph is called *bipartite* if its vertex set V can be partitioned into two sets V_1 and V_2 such that each edge in E is incident to exactly one vertex from V_1 and one from V_2. In bipartite graphs, a maximum matching can be found in $O(\sqrt{V}E)$ time due to Hopcroft and Karp [HK73]. For further algorithmic results, see Schrijver [Sch03].

Flow. A *flow network* is a directed graph $G = (V, E)$ in which each arc $(u, v) \in E$ has a capacity $c(u, v) \geq 0$. For *nonarcs* $(u, v) \notin E$, let $c(u, v) = 0$. There are furthermore two distinguished vertices in V, a *source* s and a *sink* t. We assume that for all vertices $v \in V$, the flow network contains a path from s to t including v. Further, we forbid *antiparallel* arcs, that is, we require that if $(u, v) \in E$, then $(v, u) \notin E$.

A *flow* in G is a real-valued function $f: V \times V \to \mathbb{R}$ with the following properties:

1. capacities are met: for all $u, v \in V$, we require $0 \leq f(u, v) \leq c(u, v)$.

2. flow is conserved: for all $u \in V \setminus \{s, t\}$, we require $\sum_{v \in V} f(v, u) = \sum_{v \in V} f(u, v)$.

The *value* $|f|$ of a flow f is defined as

$$|f| = \sum_{v \in V} f(s,v) - \sum_{v \in V} f(v,s).$$

A classic problem involving flows is the *maximum flow* problem. Given a flow network G, it asks for a flow of maximum value through G. The maximum flow problem can be solved in polynomial time using for example the push-relabel algorithm by Goldberg and Tarjan [GT88], which runs in $O(V^2 E)$ time.

Another well-known problem related to flows is the *minimum cost flow* problem, which is defined as follows. Let G be a flow network. In addition to the capacity, each arc also has a *cost* $\kappa: V \times V \to \mathbb{R}_{\geq 0}$ for each unit of flow passing through. The objective is then to calculate a flow through the network that has a given flow value d and minimum cost. The minimum cost flow problem can be solved in polynomial time (see for example Goldberg [Gol97]).

We can express the minimum cost flow problem as a linear program as follows. For each arc $(u,v) \in E$, let $f_{(u,v)}$ be a variable denoting the amount of flow through (u,v). We weight the flow through each arc (u,v) with the corresponding cost $\kappa(u,v)$ and minimize the total weighted flow over all arcs:

$$\text{minimize} \quad \sum_{(u,v) \in E} \kappa(u,v) \cdot f_{(u,v)} \tag{2.4}$$

$$\text{subject to} \quad \sum_{v \in V} f_{(v,u)} - \sum_{v \in V} f_{(u,v)} = 0 \quad \forall u \in V \setminus \{s,t\} \tag{2.5}$$

$$\sum_{v \in V} f_{(s,v)} - \sum_{v \in V} f_{(v,s)} = d \tag{2.6}$$

$$0 \leq f_{(u,v)} \leq c(u,v) \quad \forall (u,v) \in E. \tag{2.7}$$

The constraints ensure that the flow is conserved in each vertex (Equation 2.4), that the given flow value d is realized (Equation 2.5), and that the capacities are met (Equation 2.6). Conveniently, solutions to this (fractional) linear program are always integer if the capacities are integer, even though an explicit integrity constraint is absent [Sch03].

2.3.2 Classification

In this section we discuss the terminology surrounding classification problems. Let X be an arbitrary set called the *domain set* and call its elements *instances* (or: *samples*). Further, we call an arbitrary finite set Y the *label set* and its elements *labels* or (synonymously) *classes*. Given a domain and a label set, *classification* is the problem of deciding to which class a given instance I belongs. This decision is usually based on a finite *training set* S, which contains tuples (x,y) of an instance $x \in X$ and its label $y \in Y$, but in general does not contain I. A function $f: X \to Y$ that yields a label for a given instance is called a *classifier*.

If the label set Y only contains two labels, the corresponding classification problem is called *binary classification* and we denote the two labels by l^+ and l^-. A common approach to binary classification is based on a *score function* $s: X \to \mathbb{R}$ and a *discrimination threshold* $\tau \in \mathbb{R}$. Such a classifier labels an instance $x \in X$ with l^+ if its score $s(x)$ is greater or equal to τ (and with l^- otherwise). We say the classifier *discriminates* between instances from the two classes.

The performance of a binary classifier can be measured in various ways of which we only introduce some; for an overview, see Parker [Par11]. Consider a binary classifier with a score function s and a threshold τ, and let $T \subseteq X$ be a finite set of instances called the *test set*. We call instances of class l^+ from the test set *false negatives* if they are incorrectly labeled with l^- by the classifier. Similarly, we denote instances of class l^- that are incorrectly labeled with l^+ as *false positives*. Instances that are correctly labeled with l^+ or l^- are called *true positives* or *true negatives*, respectively. Let t_p denote the number of true positives, t_n the number of true negatives, f_p the number of false positives, and f_n the number of false negatives in T.

Then the *precision* of a classifier (on this test set) is

$$\frac{t_p}{t_p + f_p},$$

meaning the ratio of true positives to all instances classified as positive by the classifier. Similarly, its *recall* (or: *true positive rate*) is defined as

$$\frac{t_p}{t_p + f_n},$$

meaning the ratio of true positives to all instances that should have been classified as positive. The *false positive rate* is defined as

$$\frac{f_p}{f_p + t_n},$$

representing the ratio of false positives to all instances that should have been classified as negative. The *accuracy* of a classifier is defined as

$$\frac{t_p + t_n}{t_p + t_n + f_p + f_n},$$

meaning the ratio of correctly classified instances to all instances in T. Finally, the F_1 *score* of a classifier is defined as

$$2 \cdot \frac{\text{precision} \cdot \text{recall}}{\text{precision} + \text{recall}},$$

which is the harmonic mean of precision and recall.

Note that for a test set T and a fixed score function s, the quality measures defined above are still subject to the choice of the discrimination threshold τ. The quality of a binary classifier can be evaluated independently of this choice using a *receiver operating characteristic* (ROC) curve. This curve plots false and true positive rates while varying the discrimination threshold τ; look forward to Figure 3.5 for an example of such a curve. A standard method for evaluating ROC curves is calculating the *area under the curve* (AUC) [Faw06]. This value ranges between 0.5 (classification not better than a coin toss) and 1 (perfect discrimination). For a background on this topic, see Hosmer and Lemeshow [HJL04].

2.3.3 Clustering

Let X be an arbitrary finite set, and let $d\colon X \times X \to \mathbb{R}$ be a distance function over X. Given X, *clustering* is classically the problem of finding a partition C of X such that elements in the same set (called *cluster*) are near each other according to d, while elements in different sets are distant. This definition is imprecise, since it is not always clear how to combine these objectives. As a consequence, a large number of clustering algorithms with different behavior on the same input exist. Some of these algorithms require d to be a metric or the number of clusters k as input; the famous *k-means* algorithm [Llo82] for example requires both.

In this book, we repeatedly use the DBSCAN algorithm by Ester et al. [EKSX96]. It does not require prior knowledge on the number of clusters. Instead, it is *density-based*, relying on the assumption that the density of elements within a cluster is consistent and higher than outside of the clusters. This algorithm uses a slightly different definition of clustering than the one above: elements can also be identified as *noise*, that is, as not belonging to any cluster. DBSCAN requires two parameters: a real number ε defining the maximum distance between two elements to be still considered near each other, and an integer $minPts$, the minimum number of elements required to be near to form a cluster. With sufficient domain knowledge, setting these values can be considerably easier than, for example, predetermining k.

We now describe the clustering concept of DBSCAN in more detail, since we will use this terminology in Chapter 5. We start with defining the neighborhood of a point; the definitions follow [EKSX96].

Definition 1. The ε-*neighborhood* of a point $p \in X$ is $N_\varepsilon(p) = \{q \in X \mid d(p,q) \leq \varepsilon\}$.

Recall that our basic assumption is that elements within clusters are densely arranged. However, we expect that points in the interior of the cluster (so-called *core points*) have a denser neighborhood than points on the border of the same cluster (*border points*). Based on the neighborhood definition above, the following definitions formalize the concept of density while taking the different situations of core and border points into account. Each definition is with respect to given values for ε and $minPts$.

Definition 2. A point $p \in X$ is *directly density-reachable* from a point q with if $p \in N_\varepsilon(q)$ and $|N_\varepsilon(q)| \geq minPts$.

This definition is extended to pairs of points that are not necessarily within distance ε.

Definition 3. A point $p \in X$ is *density-reachable* from a point q if there exists a chain of points $p_1, \ldots, p_n$ with $p_1 = q$ and $p_n = p$ such that p_{i+1} is directly density-reachable from p_i with $1 \le i < n$.

Definition 4. A point $p \in X$ is *density-connected* to a point q if there exists a point r such that both p and q are density-reachable from r.

Based on the density-connectedness of points, a cluster is defined as follows.

Definition 5. A *cluster* C is a non-empty subset of X satisfying the following conditions:

1. maximality: $\forall p, q \in X$: if $p \in C$ and q is density-reachable from p, then $q \in C$.

2. connectivity: $\forall p, q \in C$: p is density-connected to q.

It can be noted that following these definitions, border points can simultaneously belong to multiple clusters, as long as they are density-reachable from each of them. In practice, this property is often undesired and can be changed in various ways; we use the implementation from the *Scikit-learn* library[16] which assigns border points to exactly one cluster.

Also note that not all of the input points necessarily become core or border points: points in X that do not belong to any cluster are considered to be noise. This is an advantage of DBSCAN over other clustering algorithms: it can explicitly declare points as noise if they do not fit to the identified clusters.

2.3.4 Hidden Markov Models

Consider a stochastic process defined by a finite set of *states* S, a discrete time parameter t, a prior distribution $\mathbb{P}(X_1)$ over the states at time $t = 1$, and a set of conditional distributions $\mathbb{P}(X_t \mid X_{1:t-1})$ over the current states given all previous states. At any point in time t, the process is in exactly one state $x_t \in S$. A stochastic process is called a *Markov chain* if the probability distribution over the current state is conditionally independent of any previous states except the last, that is, $\mathbb{P}(X_t \mid X_{1:t-1}) = \mathbb{P}(X_t \mid X_{t-1})$. This property is called the *Markov* property, and the distribution over the current state given the previous state is called the *transition model* of the Markov chain.

A *hidden Markov model* consists of a Markov chain M, a set of possible *observations* E, and a conditional distribution $\mathbb{P}(E_t \mid X_t)$ over the possible observations at time t given the state at time t. This distribution is called the *emission model* and only depends on the state at time t (and not on previous states or observations). The term "hidden" means that the sequence of states the system is in cannot be directly observed; instead, we obtain an observation emitted by the process at each point in time. Due to the independences

---

[16] See [PVG+11] and http://scikit-learn.org/

in this model, the complete joint distribution over all variables in the model can be expressed as

$$\mathbb{P}(\,X_{1:t}, E_{1:t}\,) = \mathbb{P}(\,X_1\,) \cdot \mathbb{P}(\,E_1\,|\,X_1\,) \cdot \prod_{i=2}^{t} \mathbb{P}(\,X_i\,|\,X_{i-1}\,) \cdot \mathbb{P}(\,E_i\,|\,X_i\,).$$

Despite the modeling restrictions, hidden Markov models are a useful tool in various applications. In particular, there are several relevant inference tasks in hidden Markov models that can be efficiently solved. For the application in this book, we are particularly interested in a maximum likelihood estimation (MLE) of the sequence of states, given a sequence of observations. That is, we want to compute

$$\operatorname*{argmax}_{x_{1:t}} \mathbb{P}(\,x_{1:t}\,|\,e_{1:t}\,).$$

This can be achieved in polynomial time using the famous *Viterbi* algorithm [Vit67].

Chapter 3

Locating Map Elements

In this chapter, we describe an efficient approach to one of the fundamental problems in information extraction from historical maps: locating occurrences of map elements such as text or place markers in a raster image. We combine template matching (to locate possible occurrences) with active learning (to efficiently filter these possible occurrences). Using this approach, we design a human-computer interaction in which large numbers of elements in a map can be located reliably using little user effort.

We experimentally demonstrate the effectiveness of this approach on real-world data, both with a statistical evaluation and in a user study. In addition, we show that our approach can be applied to other historical documents as well: we successfully use it to locate occurrences of glyphs in early printed books from the 15th century.

3.1   Introduction

Typical map elements to be extracted are place markers, their labels, and pictograms describing the physical landscape. Manually locating these elements in historical maps can be a tedious task, because even a single map can contain vast numbers of them. Historical maps can have several thousand of these elements: for example, Frederik de Wit's *Circulus Franconicus* map from 1706 contains more than 1600 labeled place markers, while the map sheet is only 55 by 47 centimeters in size. In addition, there are hundreds of pictograms showing hills or trees (indicating mountain ranges and forest areas). See Figure 3.1 for a section of this map. The manual effort required to extract comprehensive information from maps like this renders processing a larger set of maps prohibitive.

Automatically locating map elements would help to reduce the manual effort that has to be spent on extracting information from historical maps, but is difficult for several reasons. First, there is a large variation in drawing styles between historical maps, which impedes transferring methods from one map to another. Since the maps were hand-drawn, there is also considerable variance in the drawing of the same elements *within* a map; for examples, see Figures 1.3 and 2.1. The dense placement of elements in some maps can result in several pictograms overlapping, making it even more difficult to locate the individual elements. Automatically extracting semantic information from unstructured data such as bitmap images is a truly difficult task for computers to begin with. This often leads to a mediocre results when applying fully automatic approaches. However, a high detection quality is crucial, since an error in this step disturbs any subsequent analysis

---

This chapter is based on joint work with Thomas C. van Dijk and Felix Kirchner [BvD15, BvDK16].

Figure 3.1: Dense placement of map elements on Frederik de Wit's *Circulus Franconicus* map from 1706. The map section shows a multitude of settlements around Meinungen in today's southern Thuringia and is presented in its actual scale.

based on the extraction results. In light of these difficulties, we have developed an active-learning system for a generally-applicable subproblem in this area: finding approximate repeat-occurrences of pictograms. In this chapter we demonstrate that active learning is suitable for this real-world task.

As a first step, a user indicates a rectangular crop around a map element he or she is looking for, such as *◢* or *⛪*. The system uses standard techniques from image processing to find a set of *candidate matches*, but the problem remains to determine which of these candidate matches are in fact semantically correct. We model this as a classification problem and use pool-based batch-mode active learning (Section 3.3). A statistical evaluation of the proposed algorithm shows that it works well on actual data (Section 3.4). We have implemented a web-based user interface (Section 3.5) and evaluated it in a user study (Section 3.6). This study shows that the resulting human-computer interaction is effective and efficient.

Our source of maps for this chapter is the *Franconica* collection[1] maintained by the Würzburg University Library. In our experiments, we use six maps created between 1533 and 1787 from this collection. One of them is the *Circulus Franconicus* map from Figure 3.1; all other map imagery in this chapter is taken from maps of the *Franconica* col-

---

[1] http://www.franconica-online.de/

lection as well. Later in this chapter, we will also work with early typeset prints. The scans of these documents are taken from the Otto Schäfer Library Schweinfurt and the Würzburg University Library.

3.2 Related Work

Some research has gone into image segmentation specifically for bitmap images of (historical) maps. Höhn [Höh13] introduced a method to detect arbitrarily rotated labels in historical maps; Mello et al. [MCdS12] dealt with the similar topic of identifying text in historical maps and floor plans. Simon et al. [SPIB14] applied image processing techniques and a combination of different heuristics to identify toponyms in historical maps.

These systems are rather sensitive to their parameters, requiring careful tweaking in order to perform well. In a further paper, Höhn et al. [HSS13] specifically raise this as an area for improvement: their experiments work well, but do not necessarily generalize to a large variety of maps. The system of Mello et al. was developed for a large set of rather homogeneous maps, which means that it was merited to spend significant manual effort to find good parameter values. In contrast, we aim to handle more diverse maps, each with relatively small user effort. We therefore specifically address finding model parameters.

Locating Pictograms. There exist only few automatic approaches for finding elements in historical maps, and they are usually aimed at a specific corpus of maps. Leyk et al. [LBW06, LB09] introduce an automatic approach to finding forest cover in a certain corpus of 19th-century topographic maps. Working with similar maps, Iosifescu et al. [ITH16] present a system for automatically vectorizing map elements like building footprints and rivers. Giraldo Arteaga [GA13] also deals with the extraction of building footprints, in this case from fire insurance atlases from the 19th and early-20th century. We will discuss this system in more detail in Chapter 5. These approaches tend to work well, but note that they are specifically tailored to relatively recent, homogeneous maps. The tests in this chapter are performed on much older maps (16th to 18th century).

In order to detect and georeference places in such early maps, Höhn et al. [HSS13] propose a system that finds place markers and suggests possible place names based on both a modern-day map and markers that the user has previously identified. This system is based on template matching; Höhn and Schommer [HS17b] later experimented with deep learning for recognizing place markers.

Chiang et al. [CLK14] published an extensive survey focusing on the processing of more recent maps (i.e., maps from the 19th century onwards), covering a variety of image-based techniques. Such maps are of high quality when compared to older maps, since they have been designed and printed to modern cartographic standards. An example of applying image processing to such maps is the work on recognizing text in raster images by Chiang and Knoblock [CK15]. While the authors conducted experiments on modern maps only, their approach might be transferable to the much older historical maps addressed in this chapter. Dhar and Chanda [DC06] present a system that extracts geographic features from modern maps, but is based on layers of certain color rather than pictograms.

Word Spotting. A further thread of research in this direction is performed under the term *word spotting*, where the task is to locate written language in bitmap images. It is considered a positive quality if this is performed in a language-agnostic way. (Consider that humans can usually identify written text, even when unable to read the language or when unfamiliar with the font or even the script.)

Rath and Manmatha [RM07] do clustering based on connected components of "ink." It is common to apply warping techniques such as dynamic time warping (DTW) to align various copies of the same word, using *projection profiles* [RM03, MC09]. Aldavert et al. [ARTL15] study Bag-of-Word approaches for word spotting in handwritten texts. The primary concern in the word spotting literature has been the application to manuscripts, although for example Roy et al. [RPL14] experiment with labels from modern maps.

Optical Character Recognition. Another problem that requires locating repeat-occurrences of pictograms is optical character recognition (OCR), for example when applied to early typeset prints. Since off-the-shelf OCR systems do not work well on early prints due to lower printing quality and higher visual variance, general purpose OCR software like Tesseract [Smi07] and OCRopus [Bre08, BUHAAS13] has to be specifically trained. In this context, an inventory containing various examples for each glyph occurring in a given print is valuable data for training OCR engines [TDT13]. Recognizing text in early prints directly by finding repeat-occurrences of glyphs has also recently been advocated by Caluori and Simon [CS13b].

Additionally, we note that a catalog of occurrences of glyphs can in itself be interesting, for example to date or attribute printed works [Beh14]. Relying on (limited) manual effort instead of OCR, Gottfried et al. [GWL15] and Serrano et al. [SGC$^+$14] introduce interactive systems for handwriting transcription and recognition.

Active Learning. We approach the extraction of information from historical maps using active learning. (See Settles [Set10] for a survey on active learning.) In particular, we use batch-mode learning [CK13a, GS08, HJZL06]. Our approach is pool based, that is, we have a discrete set of items that we wish to classify and we can only query the oracle on those items. In effect, we learn a threshold based on logistic regression [BNG$^+$06]. See Schein and Ungar [SU07] for a general discussion of active learning for logistic regression.

The design of our system takes into account the human factors involved in using a human as oracle. This combines aspects of human-computer interaction (HCI) and knowledge discovery, as advocated for example by Holzinger [Hol13]. Such factors can be incorporated in the algorithms used, as in *proactive learning* [DC08]. For our purposes we found that standard active learning suffices.

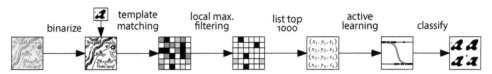

Figure 3.2: Overview of the consecutive steps in our method. The input is a bitmap generated by scanning a historical map, and a template to search for. The output is a list of positive matches and their location in the image.

3.3 System Design

In Chapter 1, we have explained our modular approach to "understanding" historical maps by creating an extraction framework consisting of small, independently operating tasks. The task we discuss in this chapter is finding pictograms and textual elements. This is an information extraction step that lifts from the unstructured level of a bitmap image to data that is combinatorial in nature: a list of locations of map elements. Figure 3.2 gives an overview of the different steps in this process.

Finding approximate occurrences of an example image is a classic problem in image processing known as *template matching* (see for example Brunelli [Bru09] for an overview). Algorithms solving this problem can be used for a variety of map elements, from place markers, to forests, to text labels: we are interested in locating repeat-occurrences of these pictograms. However, standard techniques yield only a list of candidates along with "matching scores:" this still needs to be converted into a yes/no classification. In this chapter we focus on efficiently learning a classifier in this setting.

Specifically in our application, the user provides a *template* by indicating the bounding box for an interesting map element. This could be a prototypical pictogram on the map, such as a house (⌂), a tree (🌳) or even individual characters (a, e, n). See Figure 3.3 for an example: here the user wants to find all occurrences of the character "a" and inputs the red rectangle in the leftmost image. The template matching algorithm comes up with – among thousands of others – the three matches indicated in the other images. The remaining problem is to decide which of these matches are in fact semantically correct.

The usefulness of recognizing individual characters should not be underestimated, since standard optical character recognition does not perform well when applied directly to an entire historical map: consider for example Figures 2.1c, 2.1d, and 3.1, all showing maps where the text is not clearly separated from the other map elements. Even in such messy maps, there are usually several characters that are particularly recognizable. (Which ones might depend on the handwriting.) Given one typical example of a character, our method can be used to find most of the other occurrences of the character with high precision. If we do this for a number of different characters, a later pipeline step can cluster these results to find out where the text elements are (for example: labels). This can be used as a preprocessing step for OCR, in case the OCR algorithm would otherwise get confused by overlapping map elements or is computationally too expensive to be run on the entire map. (The former is a particularly typical problem, even when applying OCR

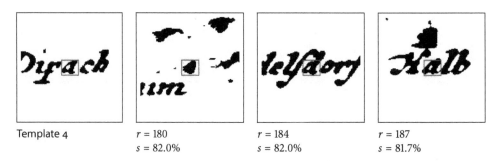

Template 4	r = 180	r = 184	r = 187
	s = 82.0%	s = 82.0%	s = 81.7%

Figure 3.3: Several sections from the same historical map. The red rectangle in the leftmost image indicates the crop used as template; the other three are computed candidate matches. Note that these three matches have similar rank and score, but do not all represent semantic matches of the template. In the ground truth we reject the rank-180 match (probably a hill) and accept the rank-187 match ("a"). The ground truth of Experiment 4 accepts the rank-184 match ("d"): see Figure 3.4 for the reasoning.

to modern maps [CK15].) This approach based on finding a small set of specific characters as preprocessing is also used by Leyk et al. [LBW06]. Because of this application, we prefer our system to have a tendency to side with precision over recall: false negatives are not a disaster if we use a suitable set of characters, since it is likely that at least some character occurrences within each label will be found.

In this chapter, we use a basic template matching algorithm, which we briefly sketch below. We deliberately chose this algorithm to show that even basic template matching leads to good results when combined with our active-learning approach. Since the elements we want to locate are all drawn with dark ink on a relatively light background, the map content is effectively black and white, and we first binarize to a 1-bit-per-pixel bitmap using a fixed threshold. (This is rather ad-hoc, but sufficient for our purpose. For a survey on proper binarization methods for historical documents, see Stathis et al. [SKP08].) Then we consider a sliding window and calculate a matching *score* for every possible position, to pixel precision: when the template is shifted to a certain position, how many pixels are equal between the template and the image, and how many are different? Following standard procedure, we take the percentage of equal pixels as our matching score.[2] This is effectively a feature extraction step, giving us a value per pixel. If the score is high for a certain pixel (that is, for a certain position of the template), it is likely that a slight shift of the template still results in a good score; we therefore discard all pixels that do not have maximal score in their 8-neighborhood. Of the remaining pixels, we select the 1000 highest-scoring ones. This cut-off is chosen generously such that all true positive matches survive this step. In this way, the template matching algorithm is used as a data reduction and projection step that takes place before the classification happens.

---

[2] Note that this basic approach is not invariant to scale and rotation. It is naturally robust against *small* variations, but some historical maps would require a more advanced template matching algorithm.

Table 3.1: Data sets used in our experiments. Each line describes one data set: the name of the map, a thumbnail of the template, characters that were considered positive matches, the area under curve according to Figure 3.5, and the self-information relative to the logistic regression model trained on all instances.

	historical map	template	accepted	AUC	self-info.
1	*Carte Topo. D'Allemagne* (1787)	*b*	b, h	0.85	462.91 bit
2	*Franciae Orientalis* (1570)	*a*	a, g, d	0.90	566.95 bit
3	*Franciae Orientalis* (1570)	*e*	e	0.87	642.02 bit
4	*Circulus Franconicus*, De Wit (1706)	*a*	a, g, d	0.92	444.48 bit
5	*Das Franckenlandt* (1533)	*a*	a, g	0.87	590.50 bit
6	*SRI Comitatus Henneberg* (1743)	*n*	n, m, h	0.92	524.85 bit
7	*SRI Comitatus Henneberg* (1743)	*e*	e	0.87	524.01 bit
8	*Circulus Franconicus*, De Wit (1706)	*a*		0.88	560.29 bit
9	*Circulus Franconicus*, Seutter (1731)	*o*		0.99	146.16 bit

All maps in this table are taken from the *Franconica* collection of the Würzburg University Library. Identifiers: **1**: 36/A 1.16-41; **2, 3**: 36/A 20.39; **4, 8**: 36/A 1.17; **5**: 36/G.f.m.9-14,136; **6, 7**: 36/A 1.13; **9**: 36/A 1.18.

This leaves the classifier. We choose to classify based on a score threshold, or equivalently: a rank threshold. A threshold that more-or-less cleanly separates the true positive matches from the true negative matches does indeed exist in our experiments: we have manually created ground truth for the templates in Table 3.1 and find receiver operating characteristic (ROC) curves with area under curve of around 0.9.

Because the maps and the templates vary wildly, picking a single threshold value for all maps and templates will not work. Some literature in fact ignores this issue (for example Höhn [Höh13]) by hand picking the value for their experiments. This is valid when the objective is to show that a certain algorithm *can* achieve high accuracy, but does not show usefulness of the method in practice. To obtain a system that is of actual practical use, we will employ pool-based active learning with a human user as oracle.

Since a given candidate match either contains the desired element (correct) or does not contain it (incorrect), we describe it with a binary variable. We then use logistic regression as a model to discriminate between correct and incorrect matches. In the experiments section we show that logistic regression is a suitable classifier when trained on complete ground truth (all labels). However, acquiring labels is the most time-consuming step in our system – it involves a human. In order to keep the necessary human effort low, we apply active learning. Following standard practice, we use the following batch-mode query strategy. As input our algorithm takes the list of candidate matches, ordered by rank, and a parameter k, the size of a batch. (We examine the choice of k in the Section 3.4.2.) The algorithm starts by assuming the best-scoring match is correct and the worst-scoring match is incorrect and (trivially) fits an initial model. Then, in each iteration it picks the k unlabeled matches that are most uncertain (according to the current model) and asks the user to label this batch; the results are stored and the model is retrained. After any number of iterations, this gives the following classifier: return the user-provided label if available, or give the most likely answer according to the logistic regression model otherwise.

3.4 Experiments

We have implemented the proposed system and applied it to several real-world data sets. This section describes our findings.

3.4.1 Evaluation Settings

We implemented our method primarily in Python, using the *Scikit-learn* library[3] for logistic regression. The template matching is implemented in C++. All experiments presented in this section have been run on a desktop PC with an Intel® Core™ i5-4670 CPU at 3.40 GHz and 8 GB of RAM running Ubuntu 14.04. Neither runtime nor memory were an issue; template matching takes up to a couple of second on practical maps and batch selection occurs in realtime.

To evaluate our active learning approach, we created nine real-world data sets. These were created by analyzing template matching results from actual historical maps, using various templates: the combination of a map and a template identifies a data set. The data sets are available online[4]; Table 3.1 gives an overview. For every data set, we considered the thousand highest-ranking matches and manually determined if they are correct. This gives us a ground truth containing nine times 1000 instances. Note that for some templates we have accepted several characters, not just the exact character in the template. This improves classification performance for cases in which the template is visually contained in the other characters; for an example, see Figure 3.4. (This is a known problem for character recognition on maps; see also Deseilligny et al. [DLMS95].) Choosing which characters to accept for a certain template currently involves some user judgment, but the sets shown in the table seem widely applicable.

The instances in these data sets have only one feature: their score according to template-matching algorithm. These scores also imply a ranking of the instances. In each of the following experiments, there was no clear difference between using the actual scores and using the implied rank. For the rest of the chapter, we report the results of using the rank of an instance as its feature.

In order to assess how difficult the classification for a particular template is, and if learning is even feasible, we use ROC analysis for binary classification with a discrimination threshold (on the rank). Figure 3.5 shows an area under curve of over 0.85 for

---

[3] See [PVG+11] and http://scikit-learn.org/

[4] http://www1.pub.informatik.uni-wuerzburg.de/pub/data/mlj16/

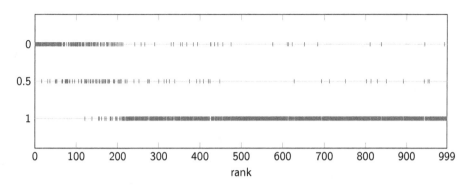

Figure 3.4: Distribution of the contents of the first thousand matches for Template 4, ordered by rank. Matches containing either "a", "d" or "g" can be separated fairly well from the remaining matches using a threshold (for example rank ≤ 200). In contrast, a discrimination of strictly the matches showing "a" will not have high accuracy.

all data sets, showing that this approach is feasible for a wide range of templates. In addition, we trained the logistic regression model on a full ground truth of each data set. This allows us to calculate the self-information (or: surprisal) for every instance, relative to this model. Table 3.1 shows the sum of self-information over all matches of each template. This can be regarded as a measure of the classification difficulty for the particular template: high self-information hints at a larger number of outliers and/or a wider interval of rank overlap between the positive and negative instances. This interpretation is confirmed by the fact that the data sets collected on maps from the 16th century have higher self-information than those on maps from the 18th century. On many of the older maps, elements indeed seem harder for humans to distinguish due to the heterogeneous style of handwriting and the suboptimal state of preservation.

We measured the classification performance of our algorithm using accuracy and F_1 score, in addition to precision and recall. Consider that for our application, precision is more important than recall: a missed character or text label might still be located later using another template, whereas false positives could potentially disturb subsequent pipeline steps (such as OCR) significantly.

3.4.2 Evaluation Results

We have run our algorithm on the nine real-world data sets introduced above and now discuss our experimental findings in terms of classification performance, runtime and parameter choice.

Classification Performance. In our evaluation, we follow the methodology proposed by Settles [Set12] and use *learning curves* to show the performance of our method. We use batch size $k = 3$ unless stated otherwise; a justification of this particular choice and a general discussion of this parameter value follows later. We compare the performance

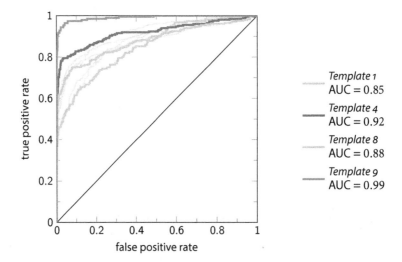

Figure 3.5: ROC curves for the data sets in Table 3.1. The labeled curves include the ROC curves with the lowest and highest area under curve for templates containing characters (Templates 1 and 4). Of the two templates for place markers, one shows typical performance (Template 8) and one performs exceptionally well (Template 9).

of our active learning strategy to a random strategy, where the batch of k samples to be labeled is picked uniformly at random from the pool of unlabeled instances. We refer to this strategy as the *baseline* and show that our active strategy outperforms it in almost every situation.

Figure 3.6 shows the learning curves of our approach in comparison to the baseline. The plots indicate the accuracy of both classifiers against the number of iterations; the number of labeled samples is three times this number, as we set $k = 3$. For the baseline, we performed 100 runs and show mean, 10th, and 90th order statistic of the achieved accuracy. The figure shows that the accuracy of the active learning strategy dominates the accuracy of the baseline at almost every number of iterations. Only in the very beginning (number of iterations below approximately 15), this is not consistently true. Still, the active learning strategy is near the 90th percentile performance of the baseline even in these situations.

In the next experiment, we consider additional performance measures. The results in this experiment refer to Template 6, as a typical example. Figure 3.7 shows the performance of our active learning strategy in comparison to three runs of the baseline. Note that after 15 iterations, the active learning classifier dominates the three baseline classifiers in accuracy, precision, and F_1 score. The baseline does better only in terms of recall, which (as discussed before) we find acceptable. The observations from this experiment also hold for a larger number of random runs and for the remaining data sets.

It can additionally be noted that, in contrast to the baseline, all four scores increase monotonically after the first few iterations when using the active learning strategy. Thus,

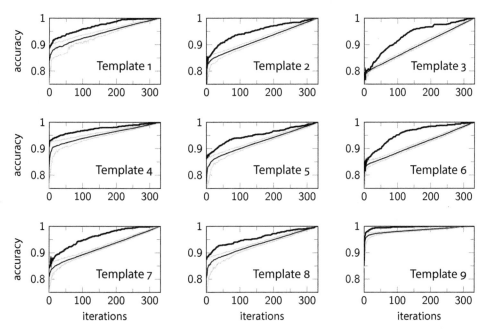

Figure 3.6: Learning curves comparing the performance of our active learning strategy ($k = 3$) to the baseline. The bold line indicates the accuracy of the active learning strategy over the iterations. The thin line shows the mean accuracy of 100 runs of the (random) baseline strategy; the gray area indicates 10th to 90th percentile.

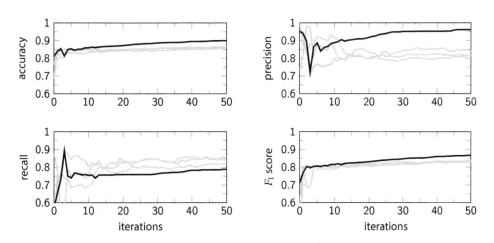

Figure 3.7: Statistics for our active learning strategy (black) and three runs of the random baseline strategy (gray) on Template 6. Note that after 15 iterations (with $k = 3$), our strategy outperforms the baseline in all measures except recall.

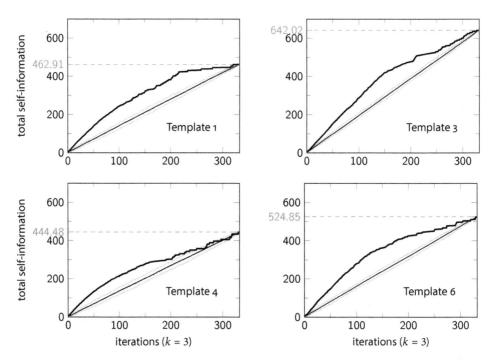

Figure 3.8: Self-information of all samples that have been labeled up to a given iteration (relative to the model in that iteration). The samples picked by the active learning strategy (bold black) are considerably more informative than those selected by the random baseline strategy (thin black: mean, gray area: 10th to 90th percentile). Note that in the end, each strategy has labeled all samples and achieves the self-information of the ground truth as listed in Table 3.1.

when additional samples are labeled, the classifier's performance is highly likely to improve. This property is especially valuable for the design of proper user interaction when using active learning: from the users' point of view, it is hard to accept that additional effort in labeling leads to a decrease in quality.

In another experiment, we consider the self-information of the samples that our strategy selects, in comparison to those chosen by the baseline. We calculate the self-information as before (Section 3.4.1), with the following small modification. In each iteration, we consider the total amount of self-information contained in all samples selected up to that iteration (relative to the model in that iteration). For almost any number of iterations, the total self-information in the samples from the active learning strategy is considerably higher than in those from the baseline. Figure 3.8 illustrates this for four templates; the same holds for the remaining five data sets. The behavior of the active learning strategy is desirable, because higher self-information means that the labeled samples were *indeed* hard to classify for the logistic regression model and therefore hav-

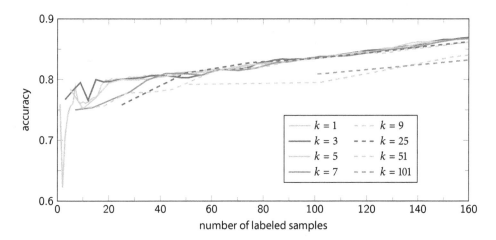

Figure 3.9: Accuracy of our active learning strategy using different batch sizes k on Template 3. For values of k between 3 and 7, accuracy is acceptable from the start and increases for increasing number of samples. Exceedingly large values ($k \geq 25$) result in inferior performance for the first few iterations and these represent significant user effort due to the batch size.

ing them labeled by the user is valuable. In contrast, the baseline selects a substantial number of samples whose labels are comparatively clear (for example because they have a very high rank), thereby wasting the user's time.

Runtime. In our decidedly unoptimized implementation, it takes a total of approximately one second of runtime to calculate 100 batches of size $k = 3$. As this represents 100 batches of user interaction, the system is clearly suitable for realtime applications. We discuss the practical runtime in the context of user experience in Section 3.6.

Choice of Parameters. Our active learning strategy depends on the batch size k. We have run experiments to evaluate the influence of k on the classification performance of our approach. Figure 3.9 shows that the performance does not depend very strongly on the choice of k, as long as no exceedingly large values are chosen. Based on this data set, we might recommend values between 3 and 7; this conclusion holds for the remaining templates.

When choosing the parameter k, human factors should also be taken into account. The time taken to decide if a displayed candidate match is correct (that is, to label a sample) varies with the batch size. Since selecting and delivering a new set of samples to the user requires a perceptible amount of time (both technologically and cognitively), a larger batch size may cause less user disturbance. For this reason – and aesthetic reasons – we currently use $k = 9$ in our web-based implementation of the user interface. We did not experiment with k in our user study because of the limited number of participants.

3.5   User Interface

We have not only evaluated the statistical suitability of our approach, but also implemented a comprehensive graphical user interface for our system. This allows us to assess
the practical applicability of our approach in a user study (see Section 3.6). In this section,
we describe our implementation and the user interfaces driven by our active learning
approach. In addition, we introduce another class of historical documents, which will
become relevant in the user study: early typeset prints. Our system can be used to find
repeat-occurrences of characters (or: *glyphs*) in this type of historical document as well.

3.5.1   Implementation: *Glyph Miner*

Our implementation of the system is available as open source software[5] under the name
Glyph Miner. The user interface is web-based (using HTML5 and JavaScript), so it can
be used seamlessly on any device that runs a modern browser. In particular, the classification interface can be used on smartphones, which enables crowdsourcing of this task.
See also Giraldo Arteaga [GA13] and Chapter 5 of this book, where we successfully apply
crowdsourcing to extract information from another set of historical maps.

Figure 3.10 shows screenshots of our implementation.[6] The interface on top allows
users to browse a historical map, crop templates and start the template matching process.
With the interface below, users can classify samples selected by the active learning system
(in the screenshot $k = 9$). By clicking on any of the nine tiles, the user indicates that the
sample is classified as positive. Once the user is finished inspecting the nine samples,
he or she presses "Next." The samples that have not been clicked on will be considered
negative and a new batch of samples chosen by the active learning system is presented.

Using the *Glyph Miner*, it takes a user with some experience approximately 25 seconds to do 4 iterations (that is, to classify 36 samples, since $k = 9$). This includes the
runtime of our active learning algorithm and client-server overhead. According to our
experimental results in the preceding section, this number of labels is already enough
to achieve reasonable classification results for a typical template. Projecting these numbers, our approach allows the effective classification of 10 templates within 5 minutes, assuming the templates have been selected beforehand. In contrast, even with significant
experience it takes about 10 to 15 minutes to generate the full ground truth for a single
template (that is, labeling all 1000 candidate matches). This leaves some time to select
the templates and still achieve a factor-10 improvement in template throughput. (Recall
that the user is probably looking for many templates on the same map.) This shows that
our system, and the proposed user interaction, is well-suited for our application. The
user study in Section 3.6 demonstrates that this also holds for users who are new to the
software.

---
[5] https://github.com/benedikt-budig/glyph-miner
[6] For a demonstration video, see https://www.youtube.com/watch?v=msJNOn7JzBw.

(a) Interface providing an overview of a historical map, a list of previously selected templates and the (unclassified) candidate matches for an "a" template.

(b) Classification interface with batch size $k = 9$.   **(c)** Classification performed on a smartphone.

Figure 3.10: Screenshots showing two user interfaces from our web-based implementation. Note that the map view (a) is intended to be used on large screens, while the classification interface (b) can be used on smartphones (c) as well.

3.5.2 Application to Early Prints

The main application in this chapter has of course been historical maps. However, our approach extends to other types of historical documents, such as early typeset prints. Like historical maps, these prints are a precious source of information for researchers of various disciplines and a remarkable part of our cultural heritage. Scans of such documents are widely available,[7] but the contained information needs to be extracted to make the most use of them. Particularly, optical character recognition is necessary to make the text contained in such documents searchable and available to further analysis. Like with historical maps, general purpose OCR systems have trouble with early prints due to lower printing quality, higher visual variation between the same characters and possibly poor conservation state of the documents.

Still, the objectives and constraints when dealing with early prints are somewhat different than when dealing with maps: instead of having a single map sheet, we are interested in finding occurrences of a given glyph in a document potentially consisting of hundreds of pages. The detected matches can then be used to create a so-called *glyph library* or to train OCR engines, both of which is of significant interest for libraries and archives that have large collections of early prints. More details on this problem and related work can be found in a separate publication [BvDK16].

Typeset glyphs in early prints are in general more similar to each other than the handwritten characters in historical maps. However, due to the extensive use of abbreviations and ligatures, the set of glyphs used in early prints is larger than in most modern prints. The use of diacritics and ligatures as well as the state of the printing technology at the time provide significant challenges for template matching. This is particularly true for so-called *incunables* (books printed before 1500), which are the oldest specimens of (European) typeset prints. Figure 3.11 shows two examples of incunables featuring a variety of demanding typesetting. The incunable on top (GW 5042)[8] was printed in Nürnberg in 1494 and contains Sebastian Brant's *Narrenschiff*. The Narrenschiff ("Ship of Fools") is considered an outstanding work in the history of German literature, being the most successful German book until Goethe's *Werther* almost three centuries later [Mäh92]. The present incunable spectacularly combines the printing techniques emerging at the time, which now poses a considerable challenge to OCR systems. Scans of this print have been used in the user study described in the next section.[9]

Our active learning system can be readily applied to such early prints. Recall that in the experiments in Section 3.4, we establish a ranking of all matches on a map according to their template-matching scores. Since early prints consist of multiple pages, we now establish this ranking over all matches located on any page. Again, we train a logistic regression model on this feature and derive a rank threshold. Note that this rank threshold

---

[7] For example, more than 17 million scanned pages are available through the Early English Books Online (EEBO) project at `http://eebo.chadwyck.com/home`

[8] Identifiers for incunables refer to the *Union Catalog of Incunabula* database, which is available online at `http://www.gesamtkatalogderwiegendrucke.de/GWEN.xhtml`

[9] These scans (and our imagery) of GW 5042 were taken from the Otto Schäfer Library Schweinfurt, see `http://daten.digitale-sammlungen.de/bsb00083146/image_11`

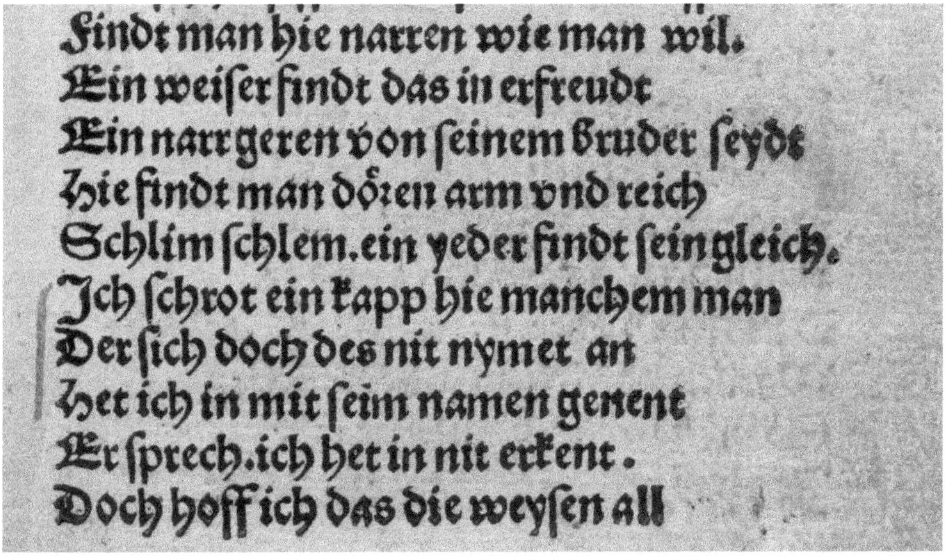

Findt man hie narren wie man wil.
Ein weiſer findt das in erfreudt
Ein narr geren von ſeinem bruder ſeydt
Hie findt man dören arm vnd reich
Schlim ſchlem. ein yeder findt ſein gleich.
Ich ſchrot ein kapp hie manchem man
Der ſich doch des nit nymet an
Het ich in mit ſeim namen genent
Er ſprech. ich het in nit erkent.
Doch hoff ich das die weyſen all

(a) *Das Narrenschiff*. Nürnberg 1494, GW 5042.

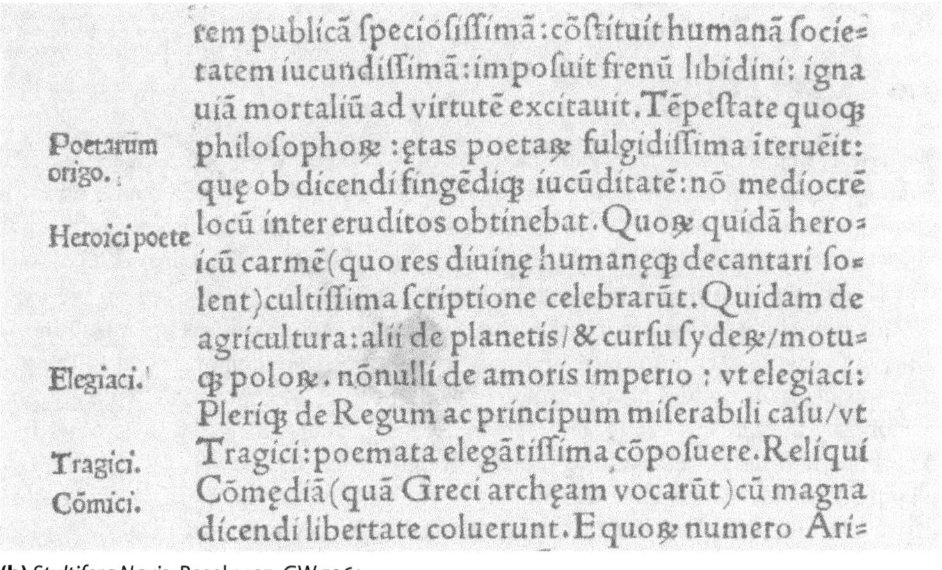

rem publicā ſpecioſiſſimā:cōſtituit humanā ſocie=
tatem iucundiſſimā:impoſuit frenū libidini: igna
uiā mortaliū ad virtutē excitauit.Tēpeſtate quoq;
Poetarum origo. philoſophoꝝ :ętas poetaꝝ fulgidiſſima īteruēit:
quę ob dicendi fingēdiq; iucūditatē:nō mediocrē
Heroici poete locū inter eruditos obtinebat.Quoꝝ quidā hero=
icū carmē(quo res diuinę humanęq; decantari ſo=
lent)cultiſſima ſcriptione celebrarūt.Quidam de
agricultura:alii de planetis/& curſu ſydeꝝ/motu=
Elegiaci. q; poloꝝ. nōnulli de amoris imperio : vt elegiaci:
Pleriq; de Regum ac principum miſerabili caſu/vt
Tragici. Tragici:poemata elegātiſſima cōpoſuere.Reliqui
Cōmici. Cōmędiā(quā Greci archęam vocarūt)cū magna
dicendi libertate coluerunt.E quoꝝ numero Ari=

(b) *Stultifera Navis*. Basel 1497, GW 5061.

Figure 3.11: Sections from two incunables printed in the late 15th century. Note the visual similarity of the glyphs **r** and **t** in the German print (a) and the extensive use of abbreviations and ligatures in the Latin text (b). Print (a) was used in our user study in Section 3.6.

(a) Viewer for early prints, showing a page on which a user selected a template for "g."

(b) Glyph Library interface, showing the set of detected occurrences of the glyph "h."

Figure 3.12: Screenshots of the user interfaces for handling early prints. In view (a), a user indicates a template using a rectangle selection tool. The interface (b) presents the current inventory of detected glyph occurrences, which can be exported for use in training OCR software.

also implies a threshold on the template-matching scores, which can then be applied to pages that were not available at training time. We have implemented these extensions of the original system in the *Glyph Miner*; screenshots of the interfaces specifically aimed at early prints are displayed in Figure 3.12.[10]

3.6   User Study

We have evaluated the *Glyph Miner* in a user study. This study was conducted at the 13th *Philtag* workshop at the Würzburg University Library and was part of a hands-on OCR session, which was attended by participants from various fields. In this session, the participants were provided with high-resolution scans of the first five pages of GW 5042, which had been binarized before with a fixed threshold.

The user study took place over approximately 45 minutes and was organized in the following way. First, the software and user interactions were demonstrated to the participants plenarily by finding an example glyph, selecting an appropriate template, and performing the active learning steps. Then, the participants received a sheet of written directions that instructed them to process five glyphs on their own. For the first two glyphs (ſ and t), the template was already in the system and the users only had to do active learning. For the latter three ("d", "e", and "y"), they were instructed to find an appropriate template on their own and then do active learning. We will refer to the first two templates as *predefined* and the latter three as *user-specified*. The participants were given 30 minutes to finish these five tasks. During this time, two supervisors were available to answer emerging questions. After finishing the assigned tasks, the participants were asked to answer a questionnaire (see Figure 3.13). This concluded the experiment.

---

[10] For demonstration video, see https://www.youtube.com/watch?v=T-p_kIdsn6k

Evaluation of Glyph Miner at philtag 13 — February 25th 2016

1 Personal background

1.1 How would you rate your prior experience...

...with Optical Character Recognition (OCR)?   none ☐ ☐ ☐ ☐ ☐ expert
...with early prints?   none ☐ ☐ ☐ ☐ ☐ expert

1.2 What is your field of work?

2 User Experience with Glyph Miner

2.1 How hard was it...

...to find templates for the requested glyphs?   very hard ☐ ☐ ☐ ☐ ☐ very easy
...to crop the templates?   very hard ☐ ☐ ☐ ☐ ☐ very easy

2.2 Template matches are computed for all pages at the same time, immediately after the "Search" button is clicked. This takes a couple of seconds. Did this wait feel appropriate?

way too long ☐ ☐ ☐ ☐ ☐ acceptable

2.3 In order to process a glyph, you have to classify a number of candidate matches (presented in groups of nine). Was the task of selecting the correct matches...

...difficult?   very difficult ☐ ☐ ☐ ☐ ☐ very easy
...enjoyable?   boring / inappropriate ☐ ☐ ☐ ☐ ☐ entertaining

2.4 You have used Glyph Miner on several glyphs. Could you imagine using it to create an entire glyph library, ...

...with respect to the amount of effort required?   not at all ☐ ☐ ☐ ☐ ☐ very well
...with respect to the quality of the results?   not at all ☐ ☐ ☐ ☐ ☐ very well

3 Suggestions

3.1 How can Glyph Miner be improved? Are any functions missing?

3.2 What did you not like?

Figure 3.13: The questionnaire that was answered by the participants of the user study.

3.6.1 Qualitative Evaluation

By the end of the user study, the participants had processed a total of 59 templates, labeled more than 5000 matches, and filled out 17 questionnaires. They worked in 16 groups of up to three members and each group shared a computer. However, due to the workshop-style setup, not all participants strictly worked through the assigned tasks. (For example, some participants selected templates for additional characters that were not asked for in the instructions.) For the evaluation of the user study, we only consider the returned questionnaires and those user actions that correspond to the instructed tasks. Our software was run on a single server and accessed by the participants through their web browsers; server performance was not an issue. Of the 17 respondents to the questionnaire, five listed "Digital Humanities" as their background, another five "digitization and OCR," and another five (German) "linguistics." The remaining two had unrelated backgrounds.

The questionnaire contained nine items that were to be answered on a five-point scale; Figure 3.14 shows the results. According to the submitted answers, the participants had varying levels of prior experience with OCR and early prints. The population size is too small to make statistical claims on the users' experience in relation to their answers to the remaining questions.

Recall that the participants were asked to specify templates for three glyphs on their own. For this purpose, they had to find the respective glyphs in the available pages and crop them using a rectangle selection tool. In the questions corresponding to this task, the majority of the participants stated that it was "very easy" to find and crop the given glyphs using the software. Each time a user inputs a new template, the template matching algorithm was run on all five pages in the sample. This process took approximately 10 seconds, which was regarded as "acceptable" by the majority of the respondents. (The two outliers arose from participants who had deficient browser environments.)

The remaining questions aim at the usability of the active learning (sub-)system specifically. During the user study, the participants had to repeatedly label batches consisting of nine matches each ($k = 9$). This activity was generally considered easy and enjoyable, even though it had to be repeated nine times for each of the five templates. The respondents judged that this effort was tolerable, even for creating a completed glyph library (which would contain roughly 100 glyphs). This was also seen in the context of the result quality, which the majority considered to be good.

3.6.2 Response Consistency

During the user study, our system was set up to log information on all user interactions. This includes user-specified templates, computed matches, and labeled samples. In addition, a timestamp for each interaction was saved. This data is the basis for the following discussion on the consistency and required user effort of our method. We measure the consistency of the users' labeling as follows. Consider all user labels available and group them according to the matches they label. For each group, count the positive and the

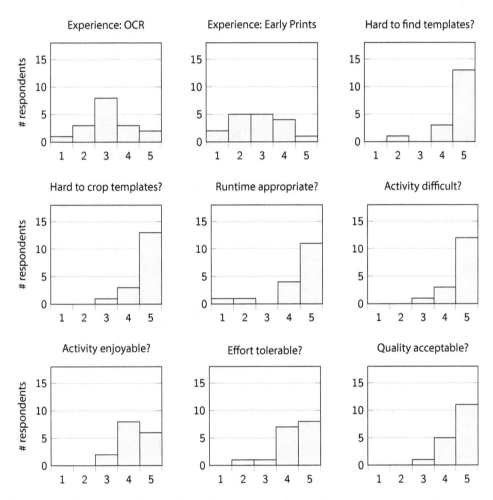

Figure 3.14: Histograms of the participants' responses to the questionnaire handed out at the end of the user study. Each of the presented questions was to be answered on a five-point scale.

negative user labels to obtain the majority vote. The *label consistency* of a group is then defined as the number of labels deviating from the majority vote, divided by the total number of labels.

While grouping the labels for the predefined templates is trivial, this is not the case for user-specified templates. First, various occurrences of the glyphs could be found and used as a template. Second, the exact size of the template depends on the individual user's judgment. This results in slight variances in the coordinates and dimensions of matches that semantically describe the same occurrence of a glyph. However, this variance is small in relation to the size of a glyph and it sufficed to cluster the matches based on their center of mass using DBSCAN (with $\varepsilon = 10\,px$ and $minPts = 1$).

We have calculated label consistency scores for the predefined as well as the user-specified templates. Restricting the groups to those matches that have at least five labels, we find that label consistency overall is high (see Figure 3.15). The ratio of matches that do not have inconsistent labels at all is above 60% for all five glyphs. For the vast majority of the remaining matches, the label consistency lies between 0.8 and 0.9; fewer than 3% have lower consistency. These outliers were mainly caused by difficulties to distinguish the glyphs "t" and "r" in our particular print (see the left part of Figure 3.11). Overall, this evaluation shows that the participants were able to label the matches presented using our method with only minor inconsistencies and, as such, can be treated as a source of fairly reliable information.

Due to inconsistencies in labeling, as well as individual choice of user-specified templates (for "d", "e", and "y"), not every occurrence of every glyph was found and correctly classified by all participants. Still, we are able to measure the *consensus* of the users on a potentially positive match in the following way. First, we again group matches with similar coordinates and dimensions as described above. Then, we consider the number of users that have classified a match as positive, restricted to those matches that were at least classified positive once (see Figure 3.16).

According to this measure, we find that for the predefined templates, the bulk of the positive matches were agreed on by at least 13 of the 15 users: 93.4% did so for "a", and 71.2% for "t." (Only few matches were identified by all 15 participants, since one participant had particularly high quality demands for accepting matches). For the user-specified templates, the numbers are similar: 89.1% of the matches are agreed on by at least 13 of the 15 participants.

3.6.3 Usage Statistics

Based on the timestamps for each action recorded throughout the user study, we can measure the time required by the participants to perform the active-learning tasks (see Figure 3.17). We find that the users were able to quickly perform the active learning step using our interface: the median time to label one batch of glyphs is 8.2 seconds. This shows that the complete process for one glyph (including template matching and active learning) can be performed in well under 2 minutes, even by inexperienced users

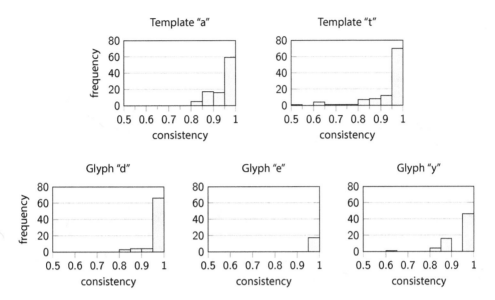

Figure 3.15: Consistency of user labels on the two predefined templates (top) and the three user-specified templates (bottom). Diagrams include all matches that were labeled at least five times. Note that by definition, the consistency is always at least 50%.

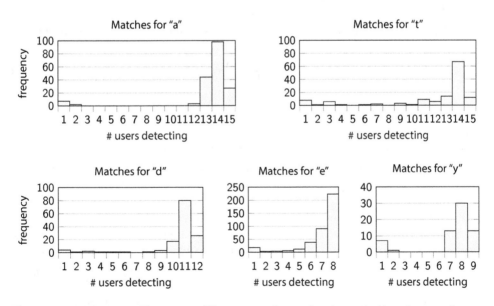

Figure 3.16: Histograms of how many different users detected each match. Note that not all users worked on all templates.

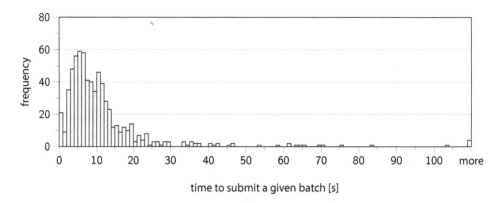

time to submit a given batch [s]

Figure 3.17: Length of time intervals required by the users for labeling a batch of nine samples. Four outliers (between 105 and 270 seconds) have been aggregated into the rightmost bar.

under suboptimal conditions, such as a crowded workshop room. A pilot study on ten computer scientists working under office conditions showed slightly better performance (compare Section 3.5.1).

3.6.4   Conclusions from the User Study

In summary, our system was well received by the participants at the workshop. The results found in the user study are for the most part transferable to historical maps as well, due to the similarity of the task. This shows the promise of applying active learning with a human oracle in practical applications – specifically for information extraction from historical documents, and perhaps also in general.

3.7   Concluding Remarks

In this chapter we have tackled a fundamental information extraction problem from a knowledge-discovery perspective: detecting occurrences of certain elements in bitmap images. We have introduced a practical approach that solves this problem in the context of scanned historical documents. Our proposed system uses template matching for feature extraction from the image, and batch-mode active learning to improve the results by finding appropriate parameter values. Particularly this active-learning step addresses an open problem in the literature on information extraction from historical maps. We implemented our approach and experimentally demonstrate that it performs well on maps relevant in practice.

In combination with the user interface we have presented, our system is able to save users a significant amount of time when examining the contents of historical maps. We have also shown that the system extends to other historical documents besides maps. In a user study, we have evaluated its practical applicability and performance in locating specific glyphs in early prints.

Directions for future work include the following. It would be interesting to exploit the potentially massive number of glyphs our approach can efficiently detect. This data could be useful for training general purpose OCR systems to recognize text both in historical maps and early prints. In particular, one could use the detected glyphs to create synthetic training data by combining them into arbitrary strings of text. (Our current implementation of the *Glyph Miner* already supports this task.) Emerging new OCR approaches based on deep learning would certainly profit from extensive sets of training data. In addition, the high detection accuracy for single glyphs reached by our system suggests that the system might be extendable into a complete OCR system.

On a more abstract level, our active-learning approach with human-computer interaction is not limited specifically to historical documents and template matching. We expect that many other computer-vision methods that depend sensitively on parameter selection can benefit from this strategy.

Acknowledgements

We thank Wouter Duivesteijn for fruitful discussion and helpful comments. We thank Hans-Günter Schmidt of the Würzburg University Library for providing real data and practical use cases. The research presented in this chapter was partially supported by the German Federal Ministry of Education and Research (BMBF), project KALLIMACHOS, reference ehuman-539-084.

Chapter 4

Matching Markers and Labels

In this chapter we present an algorithmic system for determining the proper correspondence between place markers and their labels in historical maps. We assume that the locations of place markers and labels have already been determined – either algorithmically or by hand – and want to match the labels to the markers. We model this problem in terms of combinatorial optimization, solve it efficiently, and show how user interaction can be used to improve the quality of the results. We also consider a version of the model where we are given label fragments and additionally have to decide which fragments go together. We show that this problem is NP-hard and give a polynomial-time algorithm for a restricted version of the problem.

We experimentally evaluate our algorithm on a set of historical maps published between 1533 and 1805. On average, the algorithm correctly matches 96% of the labels and is robust against noisy input. Our system furthermore performs a sensitivity analysis and in this way computes a measure of confidence for each of the matches. We use this as the basis for an interactive system, where the user's effort is directed to checking the parts of the map where the algorithm is unsure. We discuss a prototype of this system and statistically confirm that it successfully locates situations where the algorithm needs help.

4.1 Introduction

In this chapter we concern ourselves with another specific sub-task in the information extraction process from historical maps: the matching of place labels to place markers. By *marker* we mean a map element – typically a pictogram – indicating the geographic position of a point of interest. A *label* is a piece of text on the map that indicates the toponym referring to a certain marker. The question is then: which label belongs to which marker? This is in fact a nontrivial problem, even for humans. See Figure 4.1 for two examples of tricky situations that require some combinatorial reasoning in order to understand the labeling. Manually assigning labels to their corresponding markers is a time-consuming task, but provides valuable information (for example when subsequently georeferencing individual places on the map).

In the present chapter, we propose an algorithmic solution to this problem which works on various kinds of maps. We have evaluated our algorithm on medium-scale

---

This chapter is based on joint work with Thomas C. van Dijk and Alexander Wolff [BvDW14, BvDW16]. Parts of this work were developed for the author's master's thesis.

Figure 4.1: Two section from historical maps showing situations in which it is not immediately clear which marker belongs to which label. *Left:* considering the label *"Rotenbach"* separately, it could refer to any of the three markers around it. However, the constellation of the remaining labels suggest that it labels the marker on top. *Right:* a constellation with eight labels and nine markers. It is unclear which marker does not have a label.

maps published between 1533 and 1805. Like in the previous chapter, our source for these maps was the *Franconica* collection[1] maintained by the Würzburg University Library. From this collection, we have selected eight historical maps with a combined total of over 12 800 markers and labels, for which we manually created ground truth.

We discuss related work in Section 4.2. After introducing our algorithm for matching labels and markers (Section 4.3), we present several experiments that show that the algorithm performs well on the eight historical maps we have selected for testing (Section 4.4). Next, we present different extensions to this work. The first is an interactive postprocessing method that detects situations in which our algorithm was uncertain and shows them to a user for verification or correction (Section 4.5). Note that this is a different kind of interaction than in the previous chapter, where the user input was used directly to calculate a solution. Here, we are interested in identifying parts of our automatically determined solution that need human attention afterwards. We will apply the same approach to another kind of historical spatial documents in Chapter 6.

Secondly, we explore a different direction by extending our initial problem formulation to matching markers and sets of label fragments (Section 4.6). We prove that this problem is NP-hard in general, but solve a restricted version of the problem in polynomial time.

4.2 Related Work

In Chapter 3, we have presented a method for locating map elements such as place markers. In that context, we have given an overview of related work on the topic of finding individual elements; for more details, we refer back to Section 3.2. Several of the methods discussed (including our own) have been developed specifically for historical maps and

---

[1] http://www.franconica-online.de/

could be used to generate input data for the algorithm presented in this chapter. In the following discussion of related work, we focus on the detection of complete text labels.[2]

Extracting Text From Maps.   Chiang and Knoblock [CK15] present a general approach for extracting text from raster maps. Their approach is also concerned with linking detected parts of text into meaningful labels. It makes significant use of color separation for distinguishing between text labels of different kinds and other map elements. However, color separation is not applicable to many historical maps, since most features are drawn in the same color (usually black, see for example the maps in Figure 2.1). Chiang and Knoblock have only experimented with modern maps, where they report good extraction results. Based on this work, Yu et al. [YLC16] have later successfully applied an extended version of this algorithm to relatively recent historical maps from the early 20th century.

Optical Character Recognition.   Another approach to locate text labels in historical maps is the use of optical character recognition (OCR) systems. However, existing methods for OCR do not perform well on "natural scenes" such as photographs [EOW10]. This is relevant because in terms of background noise and distracting image elements, scanned historical maps can be closer to natural scenes than to the text-on-a-page setting that might be expected by OCR software.

In the context of natural scenes, Epshtein et al. [EOW10] have introduced the *stroke width transform* image operator. Their method is purely image-based and language agnostic; it does not perform OCR as such, but instead is a preprocessing step for determining *where* the text is. They report a preliminary experiment that shows that this significantly increases the performance of a subsequent OCR step. This two-step approach of first recognizing where the text is, and *then* trying to read it is quite common [CK11, NTC16].

Word Spotting Using Lexica.   Wang et al. [WBB11] report higher performance when using an integrated approach, directly looking for certain words in an image. Their approach does require a list of possible words as input (a lexicon). This may limit applicability: while they sketch several scenarios where the availability of a reasonably-sized lexicon is realistic, historical maps may not be one of them. The spelling of place names across historical spatial documents is notoriously inconsistent. (For an example, see the discussion of toponyms from itineraries in Section 2.1 and Chapter 6.)

For historical maps of Germany, one could could use the Integrated Authority File (*Gemeinsame Normdatei*, GND), which lists many historical spellings of geographic place names. For example, its alternatives for Würzburg include Wurzbourgh, Wirtzburg and Herbipolis. However, the size of this database (over 2 GB) is likely to make its use as a

---

[2] While our approach from Chapter 3 works well for individual characters, it is not trivial to combine the detected characters to obtain correct text labels. We explore this problem in the context of the present work in Section 4.6.

lexicon in the approach by Wang et al. infeasible. Another option is the use of lexica that are specialized on historical spelling variants of toponyms (for example von Reitzenstein's lexicon of Franconian place names [FvR09]). Depending on the geographic extent of the historical map to be processed, such lexica can also contain thousands of entries (see also Chapter 6).

In contrast to the approach of Wang et al., the system of Weinman [Wei13] is explicitly designed to take a large gazetteer into account. Based on probabilistic reasoning, his approach combines textual and spatial information to establish a matching between place names on the map and known places from the gazetteer. The location of the text labels on the map is assumed to be part of the input.

In summary, we note that there are several promising image processing approaches that could be used to produce the input required for our method (bounding rectangles for all markers and labels). For the best results, one should select an approach depending on the kind of maps to be processed.

4.3 Algorithmic Modeling

In our model, markers and labels are represented by axis-aligned bounding rectangles. This is a reasonable simplification on many maps, but could easily be generalized if needed (for example to rotated rectangles or arbitrary polygons). We assume these rectangles are available to the algorithm from some earlier extraction step: let P be the set of markers present on a historical map, and let L be the set of contained labels. Recall that our goal is to identify the correct correspondence between place labels and place markers. We assume that this correspondence is a *matching*: every $p \in P$ is assigned to at most one $\ell \in L$, and every $\ell \in L$ is assigned to at most one $p \in P$. However, we do not assume that there is a one-to-one correspondence: indeed, all eight maps we have tested contain unlabeled markers or stray labels. (Look ahead at Figure 4.4 for examples.) Not having the one-to-one assumption also provides robustness in case not all markers and labels were correctly identified earlier in the process.

The basis for our algorithm is the simple observation that labels are generally positioned *near* the marker they belong to. This is the basic assumption underlying our matching model. For a marker $p \in P$ and a label $\ell \in L$, we define the distance $d(p, \ell)$ as the Euclidean distance[3] between the rectangles (that is, the smallest distance between a point in p and a point in ℓ). This distance can be easily determined. In addition, we assume that labels are never located more than some distance r from the marker they belong to, which helps in deciding whether a marker is unlabeled. One could worry that this parameter r has to be chosen carefully,because an insufficiently large value might dis-

---

[3] It is also possible to use other distance measures, but the Euclidean distance (as a natural choice) already yields good results in our experiments, see Section 4.4.

Figure 4.2: Situation in which the greedy algorithm performs poorly. It returns the solid red matching $\{(p_2, \ell_1), (p_4, \ell_3)\}$, which consists purely of incorrect matches. Note that for larger values of r, the greedy algorithm would additionally match (p_1, ℓ_2) and (p_3, ℓ_4), which are also incorrect. In contrast, an optimal solution in terms of our optimization objective yields the correct matching (dashed blue). This solution does not change for larger values of r.

allow the correct matching. In practice, a suitable value is easily found: see Section 4.4.4 for an experimental discussion. Our goal is now to find a matching $M \subseteq P \times L$ such that:

(C1) M is large.

(C2) The sum of the distances in the matching is small, that is, the sum of $d(p, \ell)$ over all $(p, \ell) \in M$ is small.

(C3) No match $(p, \ell) \in M$ has distance $d(p, \ell) > r$.

We choose to minimize the sum of distances rather than, for example, to minimize the maximum distance, since in that case a single distant assignment would allow all shorter assignments to be chosen almost arbitrarily.

As a baseline for achieving these goals, we use a greedy algorithm that simply matches the closest label-marker pair and repeats, but this can perform very poorly in the worst case. See Figure 4.2 for an instance where the greedy algorithm gets everything wrong. The presented gadget can be repeated to get arbitrarily large instances with this behavior. This construction is somewhat contrived, but not entirely unrealistic. In fact, we will see in Section 4.4 that the greedy algorithm performs poorly in practice as well.

A natural way to combine our criteria into a proper optimization objective is as follows. Any pair $(p, \ell) \in M$ gives us some fixed benefit (criterion C1), but also has a cost $d(p, \ell)$ (criterion C2). We ensure criterion C3 by setting the benefit equal to r. That is, let

$$f_{\mathrm{obj}}(M) = \sum_{(p,\ell) \in M} \big(r - d(p, \ell)\big).$$

We define the LABEL ASSIGNMENT problem as maximizing f_{obj} subject to M being a matching. Note that criterion (C3) will always hold in an optimal solution since any pair (p, ℓ) with $d(p, \ell) > r$ in M decreases the objective value. The parameter r thus has another interpretation: it limits the marginal cost of adding an additional match to M.

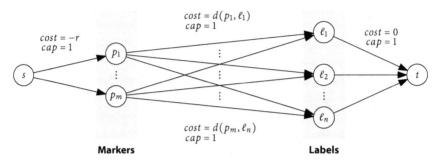

Figure 4.3: The flow network G.

An alternative to the weighted cost/benefit approach would be to consider just the costs (criterion C2) and compute a Pareto frontier [BV04] for matchings of different cardinality. We have not investigated this.

	LABEL ASSIGNMENT
Instance:	A set P of place markers.
	A set L of labels.
	A distance function $d(p, \ell): P \times L \to \mathbb{R}^+$.
	A parameter $r \in \mathbb{R}^+$.
Objective:	Find a matching M of place markers and labels such that $f_{\mathrm{obj}}(M)$ is maximized.

We solve the LABEL ASSIGNMENT problem using the flow-based approach illustrated in Figure 4.3. Let $G = (V, E)$ be a directed acyclic graph with $V = \{s\} \cup P \cup L \cup \{t\}$. It has a source s with arcs toward all nodes in P. All nodes in P have arcs to all nodes in L. Finally, all nodes in L have an arc to the sink t. With capacity 1 everywhere, this is the standard flow network to model bipartite matching [CLRS09]. We reduce our problem to a minimum cost flow problem on G by translating our maximization problem into a minimization problem and setting arc weights accordingly. Each arc (s, p) leaving s has $cost(s, p) = -r$: this corresponds to a benefit of r for establishing a match. For each arc (p, ℓ) we set $cost(p, \ell) = d(p, \ell)$: the distance-based cost. Each remaining arc (ℓ, t) has $cost(\ell, t) = 0$. Then a flow in G corresponds precisely to a solution M of LABEL ASSIGNMENT, where the flow cost equals $-f_{\mathrm{obj}}(M)$.

Finding a flow of minimum cost over all admissible flows in G gives an optimal solution for LABEL ASSIGNMENT: marker p and label ℓ are matched if and only if the flow value of arc (p, ℓ) is 1. This minimum-cost flow problem can be solved in polynomial time. Note that the standard formulation of minimum-cost flow requires a flow demand to be given as input and will minimize the cost over flows of exactly this value. Instead, we want the minimum cost over all admissible flows – of any value. This problem variant can still be solved efficiently [GT89].

Since our instances have integer capacities, we can also use (fractional) linear programming to find an optimal solution (see Section 2.3). This allows us to use off-the-shelf fractional LP solvers. It may sound unintuitive that this would be more efficient in practice, but having implemented both approaches, we found that our LP-based implementation (using CPLEX) significantly outperformed the one based on a combinatorial minimum-cost flow library (the *networkx* package for Python). The following experiments have therefore been run using the LP-based implementation.

4.4 Experiments

We have implemented our algorithm described above for experimental evaluation. The experiments have been run on a desktop computer with an Intel® Core™ i5-4670 CPU at 3.40 GHz running Ubuntu 14.04; memory was no issue. We have used Java for our implementation and CPLEX v12.5.1 for solving linear programs.

4.4.1 Data and Ground Truth

We have run experiments on historical maps from the *Franconica* collection. Some of the over 800 maps contained in this collection feature several thousand place markers. For this chapter we have manually extracted all markers and labels contained in six full maps from this collection:

- the *Franckenland* map[4] from 1533,

- the *Franciae Orientalis* map[5] created between 1570 and 1612,

- the *Nova Franconiae* map[6] from 1626,

- the *Franconia Vulgo* map[7] from 1650,

- the *Bisthum Würzburg* map[8] from 1676, and

- the *Circulus Franconicus* map[9] from 1706.

---

[4] Sebastian von Rotenhan. *Das FranckenLandt = Chorographi Franciae Orien[talis]*, 1533. Identifier: 36/G.f.m.9-14,136.
[5] Sebastian von Rotenhan and Abraham Ortelius. *Franciae orientalis (vulgo Franckenlant) descriptio*, between 1570 and 1612. Identifier: 36/A 20.39.
[6] Abraham Goos. *Nova Franconiae descriptio*, 1626. Identifier: 36/G.f.m.9-12,139.
[7] Willem Janszoon Blaeu. *Franconia Vulgo Franckenlandt*, 1650. Identifier: 36/A 10.19.
[8] Johann Heinrich Seyfried and Johann Jakob Schollenberger. *Das Bisthum Wurtzburg In Francken*, 1676. Identifier: 36/A 10.12.
[9] Frederik De Wit. *Circulus Franconicus*, 1706. Identifier: 36/A 1.17.

For two additional maps from the collection, we have extracted markers and labels from a rectangular section containing approximately 700 map elements each:

- the *Carte Topographique D'Allemagne* map[10] from 1787 and

- the *Fürstenthum Würzburg* map[11] from 1805.

This set covers nearly a three-century span of historical maps and was chosen to contain a variety of visual styles.

For our experiments, we use ground truth based on a manual matching of the markers and labels on the maps. To ensure that the ground truth was not influenced by knowledge of our algorithmic modeling, it was created by a teaching assistant who was unaware of the work presented in this chapter. He was instructed to use his best effort to resolve ambiguous cases (as opposed to making historical inquiries using external sources). All of these maps contained some unlabeled markers or stray labels. Examples of these, as well as some situations that show the limitations of our algorithmic modeling, are given in Figure 4.4. Unless otherwise noted, we have used a fixed value of $r = 150$ px on all maps. (We discuss this value in Section 4.4.4; for now, see Figure 4.11 for an indication of scale.)

4.4.2 Balanced Case

First, we have run experiments with our algorithm on *balanced* input data. This means that the ground truth data is a one-to-one assignment: this input admits a *perfect matching*. These experiments are run on a version of the ground truth where we have manually removed a small number of unlabeled markers and stray labels: as discussed above, not all historical maps admit a one-to-one assignment of markers and labels, even if our input P and L perfectly models the actual contents of the map. (The value of r is picked large enough for the algorithm to be able to find the perfect matching.) We define the *error measure* of our experiments as the Jaccard distance[12] between the set of assignments returned by the algorithm and the set of assignments from the ground truth. This definition is chosen for comparability with further experiments presented in the next section. Note that for balanced input data, this error measure is two times the precision, that is, the ratio of correct assignments to all assignments returned by the algorithm.

The filtered input data for the *Franckenland* map thus consists of 517 markers and labels. Our algorithm matches 515 labels correctly and makes 2 incorrect matches (experiment FL1). This took 0.6 seconds of runtime. On one map (*Franconia Vulgo*), the algorithm is able to assign all markers and labels correctly without making any mistakes (ex-

---

[10] Daniel Adam Hauer. *Carte Topographique D'Allemagne Contenant une Partie de l'Evêchés de Wurtzbourg et Bamberg et Fulde, les Duchés de Saxe Cobourg, Gotha, Meinungen, Hildbourghausen et une Partie de Saxe Weimar, le Comté de Schwartzbourg, le Baillage de Smalcalden, le Territoire de Schweinfurt,* 1787. Identifier: 36/A 1.16-41.

[11] Carl von Fackenhofen. *Das Fürstenthum Würzburg,* 1805. Identifier: 36/A 50.8.

[12] Based on the Jaccard index [Jac12], the Jaccard distance d_J between two sets A and B is defined as $d_J(A, B) = (|A \cup B| - |A \cap B|)/|A \cup B|$.

Figure 4.4: Examples of unlabeled markers (top row) and stray labels (middle row). The three situations in the bottom row show limitations of our modeling. On the bottom left, there are two labels sharing a common word (*"Ertal"*), thus not allowing for a matching. In the middle, a label is split in three parts that are arranged around the corresponding place marker, leading to an excessively large bounding box. On the bottom right, some labels use leaders pointing towards their corresponding markers, information that is not handled by our model. Exceptional situations like those in the bottom row occur a small number of times on each of the tested maps.

periment FV1). The algorithm performs worst on the *Carte Topographique D'Allemagne* map, where 19 of the 369 calculated assignments are incorrect (experiment CT1). Tables 4.1 and 4.2 contain these and further statistics; the experiments referred to in this section have the suffix "1."

In three of our eight experiments, the error measure is equal to or below 1%. For another three, it is below 5%. The remaining two experiments (5.4% and 9.8%) suffer from areas with particularly dense element placement, which causes the bounding boxes of some labels to overlap with each other and multiple markers. In this situation, all affected elements have distance 0 and, as a consequence, are assigned arbitrarily. Improved assignment costs $d(p, \ell)$ – not based solely on axis-aligned bounding boxes – might be able to solve this problem.

The average error measure of the experiments is 3.7%, which we consider a good result given the dense and sometimes inconsistent placement of map elements. For comparison, we have also implemented the greedy algorithm discussed before. Recall that it iteratively adds a match with smallest distance to the matching. The greedy algorithm has its smallest error measure on the *Circulus Franconicus* map (9.7%) and its highest on

Table 4.1: Statistics of our experimental results for *Franckenland* (FL), *Circulus Franconicus* (CF), *Bisthum Würzburg* (BW), and *Fürstenthum Würzburg* (FW).

experiment	FL₁	FL₂	CF₁	CF₂	BW₁	BW₂	FW₁	FW₂
# of markers	517	539	1644	1663	1150	1190	347	349
# of stray markers	—	22	—	19	—	40	—	2
# of labels	517	524	1644	1669	1150	1158	347	347
# of stray labels	—	7	—	25	—	8	—	0
correct matches	515	503	1636	1630	1123	1076	339	337
incorrect matches	2	14	8	16	27	77	8	10
corr. unass. markers	—	18	—	14	—	22	—	1
corr. unass. labels	—	6	—	22	—	4	—	0
error measure	0.8%	5.4%	1.0%	1.8%	4.5%	12.3%	4.5%	5.6%
runtime	0.6 s	0.6 s	1.7 s	1.8 s	1.1 s	1.1 s	0.5 s	0.5 s
greedy error measure	30.5%	28.0%	9.7%	10.1%	36.9%	35.4%	23.9%	23.8%

Table 4.2: Statistics of our experimental results for *Franciae Orientalis* (FO), *Franconia Vulgo* (FV), *Carte Topographique D'Allemagne* (CT), and *Nova Franconiae* (NF).

experiment	FO₁	FO₂	FV₁	FV₂	CT₁	CT₂	NF₁	NF₂
# of markers	536	549	851	868	369	374	906	925
# of stray markers	—	13	—	17	—	5	—	19
# of labels	536	538	851	851	369	374	906	907
# of stray labels	—	2	—	0	—	5	—	1
correct matches	526	517	851	848	350	342	881	871
incorrect matches	10	20	0	3	19	29	25	35
corr. unass. markers	—	7	—	14	—	2	—	15
corr. unass. labels	—	0	—	0	—	0	—	1
error measure	3.7%	7.0%	0.0%	0.7%	9.8%	14.1%	5.4%	7.4%
runtime	0.6 s	0.6 s	0.8 s	0.8 s	0.6 s	0.6 s	1.0 s	1.0 s
greedy error measure	35.6%	33.8%	14.2%	15.0%	27.2%	27.7%	28.4%	32.9%

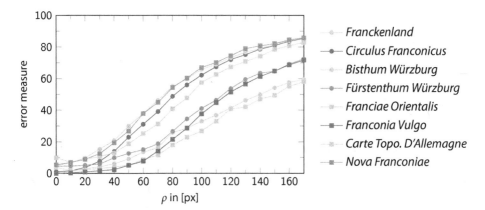

Figure 4.5: Effect of ρ on the error measure. For $\rho \leq 30$ px the graphs are nearly horizontal and below 15%. Every data point corresponds to the average error measure over 10 runs of the experiment.

the *Bisthum Würzburg* map (36.9%); its average error measure is 25.8%. We conclude that the greedy algorithm is unsuitable for this matching task, and that the results of our algorithm are indeed nontrivial. Note that the error measure of our algorithm is similar on most maps, while the greedy algorithm tends to perform particularly bad on some of the older maps (like *Franckenland* and *Franciae Orientalis*). This is likely due to the labeling style used in these maps: it requires some combinatorial inference, which our algorithm is able to do but the greedy algorithm is not.

Since our algorithm is intended for use as part of a semi-automatic digitization process, we cannot assume the input to be absolutely accurate. This is especially true for the detection of text labels, where some characters are easily missed by existing algorithms (see for example Höhn [Höh13]). In the next evaluation, we take this into account by introducing *positional noise*. Based on the ground truth data, we have shifted all labels by some offset, each label independently, uniformly at random from $[-\rho, \rho] \times [-\rho, \rho]$, for some real parameter ρ. We have then run the algorithm repeatedly with different values of ρ (10 runs per value of ρ). In Figure 4.5 we observe that our algorithm copes well with positional noise when the distances by which labels are shifted are realistic. Note that in the interval between 0 and 20 px, the error measure does not considerably increase on any of the maps. This is the width of approximately one to two characters in an average label on the maps. We consider this to be a reasonable margin for imprecision of the input. These findings also mean that the input bounding boxes do not have to exactly trace the map elements at pixel level: our algorithm is robust against some imprecision.

4.4.3 Imbalanced Case

Historical maps often contain a small number of unlabeled place markers and stray labels. Recall that this in fact holds for all eight maps we have created ground truth for. Also, when integrating our approach into a (semi-)automated digitization process, the

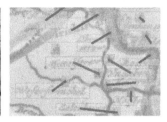

Figure 4.6: Example for an erroneous assignment in experiment CF2: the marker for *"Mittelstrew"* is matched to the label *"Unsleben"* and vice versa. The map image (left) visually suggests that *"Obrenstrew"*, *"Mittelstrew"*, and *"Unsleben"* are each labeled across the river. This assumption can be confirmed by modern map data, since the three villages still exist. Considering the manually created bounding boxes (center), the distances between markers and labels caused by the river become apparent. This, together with the crowdedness of the area, causes the algorithm to fail: it assigns labels vertically along the river rather than across it (right). Also note the unlabeled marker above the *"Mittelstrew"* label.

preceding steps might have missed some of the map elements entirely. In the upcoming experiments, we assess the performance of our algorithm in such situations. Again we use the manually-created ground truth for the eight maps, but this time we do not filter P and L to obtain a one-to-one assignment. Instead, we use the unmodified ground truth that exactly reflects the contents of the maps.

In this setting, possible errors include unlabeled markers and stray labels that are falsely assigned to another map element (instead of being left unmatched). In addition, map elements that do have a corresponding element may erroneously be left unmatched by the algorithm. Note that both of these error types are reflected by our error measure.

The input data based on the *Franckenland* map in this version contains 539 markers and 524 labels; according to the ground truth, 22 markers and seven labels do not have a counterpart. Our algorithm gives a matching of size 517, which contains 503 correct matches (experiment FL2). Of the 14 incorrect matches, four assign markers that are actually unlabeled and one assigns a stray label. The remaining nine incorrect assignments involve only place markers and labels that have counterparts. Conversely, six out of seven stray labels and 18 out of 22 unlabeled markers are correctly left unassigned. Taking all errors into account, we get an error measure of 5.4%, with a runtime of 0.6 s (which is the same as in the balanced case).

Doing the same for the *Circulus Franconicus* map, we have an input of 1663 markers and 1669 labels, with 19 unlabeled markers and 25 stray labels. The error measure in this experiment (experiment CF2) is 1.8%, with a runtime of 1.8 s. Note that the error measure on this map is considerably lower than on the *Franckenland* map. As discussed in Section 4.4.2, the labeling in that map has a more complex structure, which is further complicated by including the stray map elements.

The experiments on the remaining maps show similar results (error measures on average 6.8%), with the *Carte Topographique D'Allemagne* again being worst (14.1%). On

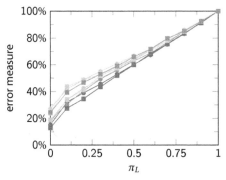
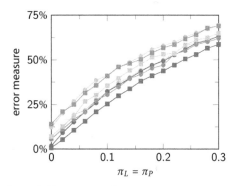

Impact of π_L on the error measure (with $\pi_P = 0.1$)   Impact of $\pi_P = \pi_L$ on the error measure

Figure 4.7: Impact of randomly removing labels and markers on the error measure in different settings. For a legend to the plots, see Figure 4.5.

all maps, error measures are higher than for the balanced case, but we still consider the results to be of high quality. The greedy algorithm performs poorly in this imbalanced setting as well, returning matchings with an average error measures of 25.8%. Further statistics are provided in Tables 4.1 and 4.2; the experiments referred to in this section have the suffix "2." Figure 4.6 shows an example of an incorrect assignment returned by our algorithm in this set of experiments.

The setting in the imbalanced case allows us to address imprecision in the input beyond positional noise: missing elements. We tested this scenario on artificial instances, starting with the ground truth and removing each element from P with probability π_P and each element from L with probability π_L. In several experiments, we varied values for both probabilities (see Figure 4.7). On all maps, error measures immediately increase with π_P and π_L: even with low values for these probabilities, the errors are not mitigated by the algorithm. This is not surprising, as the benchmark is not fair: the algorithm simply cannot match map elements that it does not know about, but is still scored against the full ground truth. Assuming that a previous processing step has failed to detect such elements, this experiment reflects a realistic setting. This effect is in contrast to the positional noise, where some noise was tolerated. Still, the algorithm is able to correctly identify the *resulting* situation, where some labels and markers have become unmatchable. With increasing deletion probability, the number of correct matches decreases linearly, but the error measure in the remaining instance is almost unaffected: missing some elements does not significantly "confuse" the algorithm.

4.4.4 Parameter Choice

The quality of the matching relies to some extent on a reasonable choice of the parameter r: our algorithm will not assign labels that belong to markers with distance greater

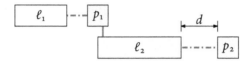

Figure 4.8: When using parameter $r < d$, the marker p_2 is too far away from label ℓ_2 to be considered. This results in the matching $\{(p_1, \ell_2)\}$. With a higher value of r, the presumably correct matching $\{(p_1, \ell_1), (p_2, \ell_2)\}$ is found.

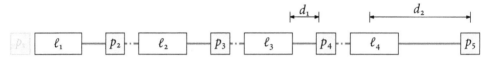

Figure 4.9: A situation in which increasing r leads to an incorrect matching. Assume that p_1 exists on the map, but was not correctly detected and is thus not part of the input. Also assume that p_5 is unlabeled on the actual map. For $r = d_1$, our algorithm returns the correct matching $\{(p_2, \ell_2), (p_3, \ell_3), (p_4, \ell_4)\}$ (dashed blue). In contrast, for $r = d_2$, our algorithms "flips" those matches and returns the entirely incorrect matching $\{(p_2, \ell_1), (p_3, \ell_2), (p_4, \ell_3), (p_5, \ell_4)\}$ (solid red).

than r. Due to the combinatorial nature of the problem, this can also influence the assignment of markers and labels that are less than r apart (see Figure 4.8). Picking a value of r that is too low can clearly be a problem in this way. Less intuitively, r can also be too high: one can construct instances such that our algorithm has an error measure of 0% for some r and 100% for a higher r (see Figure 4.9 for an example). However, such instances can be considered pathological.

We have experimentally evaluated the effect of r on the error measure for our set of eight historical maps. Using balanced input data and fixed positional noise $\rho = 40$ px, we see that the error measure does not increase significantly for high values of r (Figure 4.10). Even for an excessively large $r = 1000$ px, the error measure stays at approximately the same level as for $r = 150$ px. In contrast, picking a value for r that is too small (in this case, below 60 px) does lead to many errors.

Arcs in the flow network with cost larger than r cannot be part of an optimal solution and can therefore be excluded when running the algorithm. In this way, a low value of r leads to a lower runtime since the flow network G is smaller. With $r = 150$ px, our algorithm runs experiment CF1 in 2.1 seconds; with $r = 1000$ px, this increases to 11.9 seconds, even though the algorithm finds the exact same matching. This illustrates that r should not be set arbitrarily high.

A reasonable value for r can usually be determined visually by a user before running the algorithm. For example, we arrived at $r = 150$ px by observing that the distance between a label and the corresponding marker in our test maps is typically limited to 2 or 3 times the average text height (Figure 4.11) and picking r larger by a significant margin. The dense placement of elements in some maps (for example *Circulus Franconicus*) would also allow a lower value of r without affecting the returned matching, for example $r = 100$ px.

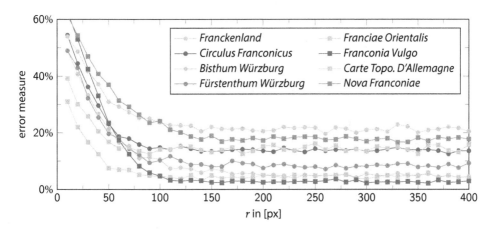

Figure 4.10: Effect of r on the error measure ($\rho = 40\,$px). Every data point corresponds to the average error measure over 10 runs of the experiment.

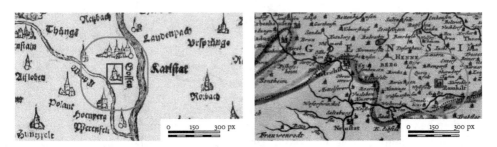

Figure 4.11: Value of r on *Franckenland* (left) and *Circulus Franconicus* (right). The red boundary marks a distance of 150 px from the blue bounding box. For both maps, this corresponds to a distance of approximately 1 cm on the map sheet.

4.5 Smart User Interaction

In general, historical maps can contain situations where it is unclear (even to a human reader without domain knowledge) how the markers and labels belong together. This is also the case with the maps used in our experiments. Changing a single match in such situations can propagate to other matches. Figure 4.12 shows an example where three distinct matchings seem reasonable: the correct matching is unclear without additional topographic or historical information.

Figure 4.13 shows a screenshot of our prototype plug-in[13] for the open-source geographic information system QGIS.[14] Our tool automatically presents areas of the map that the algorithm is most unsure about and asks the user for confirmation. (How these

---

[13] https://github.com/benedikt-budig/historical-sensitivity-plugin
[14] http://www.qgis.org/

Figure 4.12: A difficult case: without geographic or historical context it is hard to tell which one of these three matchings is correct.

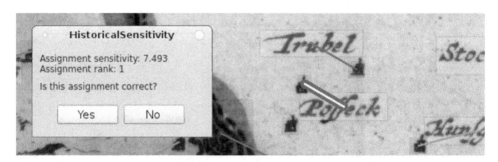

Figure 4.13: Screenshot of our prototype for interactive postprocessing. The white/blue matching on the map is presented to the user for verification.

areas are picked is described after the example.) The user's confirmation or correction can then be taken into account for a new run of the algorithm. Note that the indicated assignment in Figure 4.13 is indeed unclear. There are three markers near the label "*Posseck*" and one clearly belongs to the label "*Trubel*": the algorithm assigns this correctly. For lack of another reasonable label, however, one of the two remaining markers must remain unlabeled. Purely from the image it is unclear which one, so a user with domain knowledge must get involved.

Since a typical map in our data set contains hundreds to thousands of map elements, it is not practical to show every single match to the user for verification. Instead, we perform a sensitivity analysis of each match (p, ℓ) and develop a classifier to determine which matches warrant user inspection.

We use the following sensitivity analysis. Starting with an optimal solution M (to LABEL ASSIGNMENT), we calculate for each $(p, \ell) \in M$ how much more expensive we could make that arc without changing the optimum – equivalently: how much worse does the objective value get if we were not allowed to use (p, ℓ)? If this difference is large, then we can have some confidence in this particular match: all matchings that do not contain this match are much worse. If, on the other hand, the difference is small, then there are alternative matchings that the algorithm would consider almost as good as M: if the input were just slightly perturbed, perhaps one of those other matchings would be considered best. Then we call the match (p, ℓ) *sensitive* and decide that it is best to get a judgment from the user, since the algorithm does not inspire confidence.

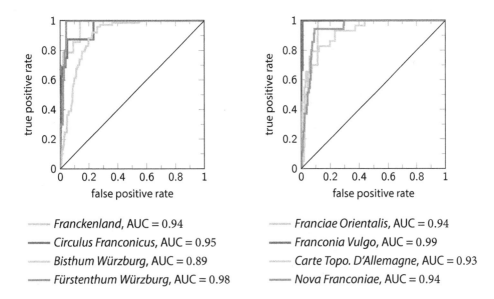

Franckenland, AUC = 0.94
Circulus Franconicus, AUC = 0.95
Bisthum Würzburg, AUC = 0.89
Fürstenthum Würzburg, AUC = 0.98

Franciae Orientalis, AUC = 0.94
Franconia Vulgo, AUC = 0.99
Carte Topo. D'Allemagne, AUC = 0.93
Nova Franconiae, AUC = 0.94

Figure 4.14: ROC curves for classifying matches by sensitivity.

This leaves the classifier. Based on the sensitivity values, we want to classify the assigned pairs in M into INSPECT and ASSUME CORRECT. The latter should all be correctly assigned (so all mistakes get caught) and the former should all be wrong (so as to not waste the user's time). We use a binary classifier with a discrimination threshold τ that simply sorts the matches in order of sensitivity and presents the τ most sensitive to the user for inspection. This parameter (based on a number of matches, rather than an objective value) is a reasonable measure for the amount of user effort we wish to expend and fits well to the standard receiver operating characteristic (ROC) analysis that we will perform on this classifier.

We have run our classifier on the optimal assignments for the eight data sets from Section 4.4 (with imbalanced input). To evaluate the performance of the classifier, we calculated the ROC curve using the ground truth data; see Figure 4.14. The area under curve (AUC) in our experiments lies between 0.89 for the *Bisthum Würzburg* map and 0.99 for the *Franconica Vulgo* map. Generally an AUC value between 0.8 and 0.9 can be considered excellent, while values over 0.9 are outstanding [HJL04]. This shows that our classifier successfully finds problematic areas.

In our implementation, we use CPLEX's *warm start* feature to speed up the computation of the sensitivities. This uses partial results from the computation of M when determining how the optimal matching changes when a certain match is disallowed.[15] This speeds up the process since the new matching is probably close to M. (Disallow-

---

[15] Using a previously computed solution to quickly solve similar instances is a common technique when using the simplex algorithm. This is widely supported by linear programming software.

ing a single match is likely to have local effects only.) Note that there exist also other approaches for calculating the sensitivity values, for example a combinatorial algorithm by Liu and Shell [LS11].

The runtime of our implementation for calculating the sensitivities and running the classifier was 1.2 seconds for our smallest instance (*Fürstenthum Würzburg*) and 46.3 seconds for the largest (*Circulus Franconicus*); without a warm start the latter takes almost an hour. For the other maps, runtimes were in between these two values.

Next, we examine the robustness of our classifier by introducing errors to our test input: we randomly remove map elements as discussed in Section 4.4.3. As an example, we conduct this experiment on the *Franckenland* and the *Circulus Franconicus* map. Removing 10% of the markers and up to 30% of the labels, the AUC value of our classifier stays above 0.8 on both maps. Based on balanced input but with introduced positional noise, the AUC is above 0.8 with ρ up to 70 px. For an extreme value of $\rho = 150$ px, the AUC value is still above 0.7 for the *Franckenland* map and above 0.6 for the *Circulus Franconicus* map. These experiments show that our classifier is sufficiently robust against erroneous input data to be of practical value.

By running the sensitivity analysis, we obtain for each match $(p, \ell) \in M$ an alternative matching, namely a matching M' that is optimal subject to $(p, \ell) \notin M'$. When presenting an unclear match (p, ℓ) to the user, we can immediately show this matching: the best alternative matching if (p, ℓ) is indeed incorrect. Figure 4.15 shows an example of how the sensitivity analysis could be presented to the user. The depicted map contains the unclear situation from Figure 4.12, with the sensitivity values color coded from red to green. These matches have indeed been identified by the classifier and are displayed as uncertain by our sensitivity analysis. The figure also shows how we could instantly preview the next-best matching to the user in case he or she considers rejecting a match (here the match under the mouse pointer). In the depicted situation, the next-best matching would only differ on three edges (dashed blue).

Also note that the values obtained from the sensitivity analysis can be stored and used in later steps. For example, Chiang [Chi15] requests such information as an "accuracy estimate" for the resulting output. Similarly, Herold et al. [HKN+17] propose to store metadata describing the information extraction process together with the results; extraction accuracy is a highly relevant information in this context.

4.6 Label Fragments

In the preceding section we have presented a way to improve the quality of matching results by including user feedback. Next, we discuss a different approach to improve matching results based on refining our optimization model. We observe that state-of-the-art label detection often detects parts of text that belong to a single label as separate labels. This is for example the case with the label detection approaches by Höhn [Höh13] and Yu et al. [YLC16] (as well as in our preliminary experiments with other approaches).

Figure 4.15: Color-coded visualization of our system's confidence in each match. An alternative is presented for the match under the mouse pointer. Note that the unclear situation from Figure 4.12 has been identified and highlighted in red.

See the map in Figure 4.16 for an example from our own experiments. Some of these label fragments clearly belong together and should have been detected as one (for example ℓ_1, ℓ_2, and ℓ_3): this is a mistake by the label detection. Then again, on some historical maps it occurs that multiple fragments of text together form a single logical label. Consider the fragments ℓ_9 and ℓ_{10}. They are geometrically separated by a place marker, but *together* form its label "*Unt. Walbering.*" For more examples, refer back to the map in Figure 2.1b (on page 13). This map has many such split labels, some even broken vertically into multiple lines, such as "*Hai-*" and "*delfelt*" in the middle left. Still, separately detected label fragments that form one logical label are located relatively close to each other (and to the corresponding place marker). We use this property to improve our matching results by adapting the LABEL ASSIGNMENT problem accordingly.

In order to generate the input for our algorithm, we are interested in identifying label fragments that might form a single label on the map. For this purpose, we propose using a heuristic that constructs a family of sets containing fragments that possibly belong together. For instance, such a heuristic could put label fragments that are located within a certain distance from each other into one set. On maps that contain mostly horizontal text, one might want to restrict the elements of a set to fragments that are aligned horizontally. In fact, Yu et al. [YLC16] present a similar heuristic for label fragments on 19th-century maps. The list on the right of Figure 4.16 shows an example of a family $\mathcal{F}$ of sets that a heuristic could return in the given map situation. Note that we al-

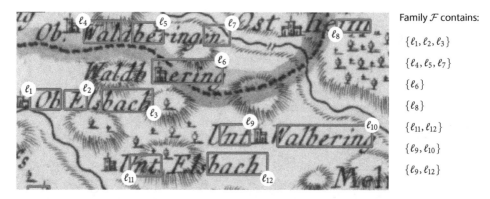

Family $\mathcal{F}$ contains:

$\{\ell_1, \ell_2, \ell_3\}$

$\{\ell_4, \ell_5, \ell_7\}$

$\{\ell_6\}$

$\{\ell_8\}$

$\{\ell_{11}, \ell_{12}\}$

$\{\ell_9, \ell_{10}\}$

$\{\ell_9, \ell_{12}\}$

Figure 4.16: Label fragments detected with a prototype label-detection algorithm. Note that many labels have (incorrectly) been detected as several separate fragments. On the right, we give an example family of sets that indicates which fragments might belong together. Note that it includes both $\{\ell_9, \ell_{12}\}$ and $\{\ell_{11}, \ell_{12}\}$.

low fragments to be contained in more than one set to deal with unclear situations, such as for example the constellation of ℓ_9, ℓ_{10}, and ℓ_{12} in the lower right. (We will discuss a restricted formulation where each label fragment is contained in only one set in Section 4.6.4.) Label fragments that do not have other fragments in their immediate vicinity could as well be the only element in a set, such as ℓ_8.

4.6.1 Optimization Problem

Given a family of sets $\mathcal{F}$, we assume that all elements ℓ in a set $S \in \mathcal{F}$ could, together, plausibly form a single label. If they do, this entire set should be assigned to a single place marker. One could try to model this problem by directly matching place markers to sets in $\mathcal{F}$. We take a different approach and extend the LABEL ASSIGNMENT formulation from Section 4.3: we again calculate a matching between markers and label (fragments) taking the information from $\mathcal{F}$ into account. We will not necessarily find a matching that includes all label fragments. Instead, our problem formulation favors matching only one fragment per set in $\mathcal{F}$, and we interpret this as matching the entire set. We will discuss this interpretation in more detail after giving the problem statement; for an example, look ahead at Figure 4.17c.

Recall the three desiderata for a matching M as introduced in Section 4.3:

(C1) M is large.

(C2) The sum over $d(p, \ell)$ for all $(p, \ell) \in M$ is small.

(C3) No match $(p, \ell) \in M$ has distance $d(p, \ell) > r$.

Since we assume that the label fragments within a set S actually form a single label on the map, we would like to match only one fragment in S to a place marker (and then

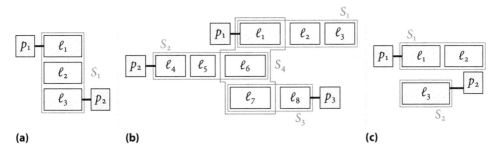

Figure 4.17: Three different situations and the corresponding solutions to the Fragment Assignment problem. In situation (a), the assignment of label fragment ℓ_2 remains ambiguous; likewise in (b), the assignment of ℓ_6 and ℓ_7 is ambiguous (consider S_4). The solution in situation (c) yields a unique assignment and avoids splitting S_1.

assume that the remaining fragments in S belong to the same marker). In other words, we do not want to split a set S by assigning its fragments to multiple place markers. We add a fourth goal which takes this into account:

(C4) At most one label fragment ℓ from each $S \in \mathcal{F}$ should be matched in M.

This is not a hard constraint, but instead something we try to avoid through optimization. We combine these four goals into a new objective function by introducing a penalty term for any sets that get split:

$$g_{\text{obj}}(M) = \sum_{(p,\ell) \in M} (r - d(p, \ell)) - \sum_{S \in \mathcal{F}} c(S, M) \tag{4.1}$$

where $c: \mathcal{F} \times 2^L \to \mathbb{R}_{\geq 0}$ is a function that applies a penalty φ for each match beyond the first from each set S as follows:

$$c(S, M) = \begin{cases} 0 & \text{if } S \cap M = \varnothing, \\ \varphi \cdot (|S \cap M| - 1) & \text{otherwise.} \end{cases} \tag{4.2}$$

We want to maximize g_{obj} under the constraint that M is a matching. By choosing a positive value for the penalty φ, each match $(p, \ell) \in M$ with $\ell \in S$ lowers the matching value if M contains at least one other match (p', ℓ') with $\ell' \in S$. We call minimizing this new objective g_{obj} the FRAGMENT ASSIGNMENT problem.

Solving the FRAGMENT ASSIGNMENT problem does not immediately give a matching between *all* label fragments and place markers. See Figure 4.17 for three example situations. In situation (a), we have the optimal matching $\{(p_1, \ell_1), (p_2, \ell_3)\}$. Since this matching splits S_1, it is uncertain which of the two place markers the remaining fragment ℓ_2 belongs to. In situation (b), the optimal matching is $\{(p_1, \ell_1), (p_2, \ell_4), (p_3, \ell_8)\}$. This only assigns the label fragments ℓ_1, ℓ_4, and ℓ_8. Based purely on the sets in $\mathcal{F}$, it is ambiguous whether ℓ_6 is part of the label for p_1 or p_2 (and whether ℓ_7 belongs to p_2

or p_3). Situation (c) shows that our optimization goal actually makes sense: p_2 is closer to ℓ_2, but is assigned to ℓ_3 to avoid (the costs of) splitting S_1.

Although we do not necessarily find a matching of all fragments, we still obtain useful information: a set of *reasonable* assignment options for each fragment. This could for example be used in a user interaction or as the input of a postprocessing heuristic. Considering situation (b) again, fragment ℓ_6 could be presented to the user with the suggestion that it belongs to either p_2 or p_1. For fragment ℓ_3, the only reasonable options are matching it to p_1 or leaving it unmatched.

4.6.2 Integer Linear Program

The FRAGMENT ASSIGNMENT problem is NP-complete, as we will show in Section 4.6.3. Here we present an integer linear programming formulation for the problem. Let $x_{p,\ell} \in \{0,1\}$ be a decision variable that indicates whether (p, ℓ) is taken into the matching or not – that is, we let $M = \{(p, \ell) \mid x_{p,\ell} = 1\}$. Additionally, for each $S \in \mathcal{F}$, we introduce an auxiliary variable $y_S \in \mathbb{Z}_{\geq 0}$ to track if multiple elements of S are part of the matching M: we use this to apply the proper splitting penalties to the objective function. For notational convenience, let $w(p, \ell) = r - d(p, \ell)$. Note that $w(p, \ell)$ and φ are constants. We can now use the objective function from Equation (4.1) to formulate the following integer linear program.

$$\text{maximize} \quad \sum_{p \in P} \sum_{\ell \in L} x_{p,\ell} \cdot w(p, \ell) - \sum_{S \in \mathcal{F}} y_S \cdot \varphi \qquad (4.3)$$

$$\text{subject to} \quad \sum_{p \in P} x_{p,\ell} \leq 1 \qquad \forall \ell \in L \qquad (4.4)$$

$$\sum_{\ell \in L} x_{p,\ell} \leq 1 \qquad \forall p \in P \qquad (4.5)$$

$$\sum_{\ell \in S} \sum_{p \in P} x_{p,\ell} \leq 1 + y_S \qquad \forall S \in \mathcal{F} \qquad (4.6)$$

$$x_{p,\ell} \in \{0,1\} \qquad \forall p \in P, \ell \in L \qquad (4.7)$$

$$y_S \in \mathbb{Z}_{\geq 0} \qquad \forall S \in \mathcal{F}. \qquad (4.8)$$

Constraints (4.4) and (4.5) ensure that the each marker and each label fragment is assigned at most once. Together this guarantees that M is a matching. Constraint (4.6) forces y_S to be at least the number of matches within S minus one, thus applying the penalty to the objective value: in particular, if S is not split, then y_S can be set to o in order to get no penalty.

4.6.3 NP-Hardness

We will now show that optimizing g_{obj} is NP-hard. Our proof uses a polynomial-time reduction from the NP-complete Set Packing problem to a decision variant of the Fragment Assignment problem; the following definition is taken from Karp [Kar72].

Set Packing

Instance: A family of sets $\{S_j\}$.

A positive integer k.

Question: Does $\{S_j\}$ contain k mutually disjoint sets?

We take the following natural decision variant of our problem to reduce to.

Fragment Assignment

Instance: A set P of place markers.

A set L of label fragments with $|L| \geq |P|$.

A weight function $w(p, \ell): P \times L \to \mathbb{R}_{\geq 0}$.

A family $\mathcal{F} \subseteq 2^L$.

A cost function $c(S, M): \mathcal{F} \times 2^L \to \mathbb{R}_{\geq 0}$.

A threshold θ.

Question: Does there exist a matching M of place markers and label fragments such that $g_{obj}(M) \geq \theta$?

Theorem 4.1. *The* Fragment Assignment *problem is NP-complete.*

Proof. First we note that Fragment Assignment is clearly in NP. We show hardness by reducing the classic Set Packing problem to Fragment Assignment.

(*Reduction.*) We construct the following Fragment Assignment instance in polynomial time. Let the set of label fragments L be $\bigcup_j S_j$. Let $\mathcal{F}$ be the family of sets $\{S_j\}$. We introduce k place markers (which form the set P) and let $w(p, \ell) = 1$ for all $p \in P$ and $\ell \in L$. Let $\theta = k$. For $c(S, M)$, we use the function from Equation (4.2) with $\varphi = 1$.

(*Equivalence.*) Assume $\{S_j\}$ contains k mutually disjoint sets. Then there are also k mutually disjoint sets of label fragments in $\mathcal{F}$. Matching each of the k place markers to an arbitrary label fragment from a different disjoint set in $\mathcal{F}$ yields a solution M for Fragment Assignment with $g_{obj}(M) = k$: since at most one element from each set in $\mathcal{F}$ was matched, no penalties were applied.

For the other direction, suppose there is a solution M to the Fragment Assignment instance such that $g_{obj}(M) \geq \theta = k = |P|$. Then every marker is matched and no sets are split: $\{S_j\}$ contains k mutually disjoint sets. □

4.6.4 Polynomial-Time Algorithm for a Restricted Problem

Since solving FRAGMENT ASSIGNMENT on large instances is not feasible, we focus on a restricted version of the problem. Recall that in the general version of the problem as stated above, label fragments can be element of more than one set. If we instead require that each fragment is contained in only one set – that is, that $\mathcal{F}$ is a partition of L – we can give a polynomial-time algorithm for this restricted problem, which we call FRAGMENT ASSIGNMENT (DISJOINT SETS).

	FRAGMENT ASSIGNMENT (DISJOINT SETS)
Instance:	A set P of place markers.
	A set L of label fragments with $|L| \geq |P|$.
	A weight function $w(p, \ell): P \times L \to \mathbb{R}_{\geq 0}$.
	A partition $\mathcal{F}$ of L.
	A cost function $c(S, M): \mathcal{F} \times 2^L \to \mathbb{R}_{\geq 0}$.
Objective:	Find a matching M of place markers and label fragments such that $g_{\text{obj}}(M)$ is maximized.

Note that FRAGMENT ASSIGNMENT (DISJOINT SETS) is still able to yield useful results in practice: the algorithm is able to correctly solve the situations in Figure 4.17c as well as in Figure 4.17a, since the formulation still allows to split fragment sets if necessary.

Requiring a partitioning of the label fragments is reasonable in many situations. As an example, in the situation in Figure 4.16, we can easily find a partition of detected fragments that are likely to belong together. This is especially the case under the assumption that detected text areas belong together horizontally, for example if a label has been split by another map element (like a river or a place marker). We can meet this new requirement by applying a different heuristic to the label fragments of the input, which clusters them into disjoint sets. This can for example be done by applying standard clustering algorithms such as DBSCAN.

We can solve the FRAGMENT ASSIGNMENT (DISJOINT SETS) problem efficiently by augmenting the flow network introduced for solving the ASSIGN LABELS problem (Section 4.3). For every set $S \in \mathcal{F}$, we introduce a *set gadget* to the flow network; Figure 4.18 shows its structure. The construction guarantees that one unit of flow can pass the gadget without increasing costs, whereas each additional unit of flow increases total costs by φ. The number of flow units that enter each gadget is equal to the number of label fragments in S that were matched. This corresponds directly to the behavior of the cost function $c(S, M)$ defined in Equation (4.2). The augmented flow network thus correctly models the FRAGMENT ASSIGNMENT (DISJOINT SETS) problem.

The gadget for set i consists of two additional vertices, g_i^{in} and g_i^{out}. The entrance vertex g_i^{in} can be reached from all label fragments that belong to the set corresponding to the

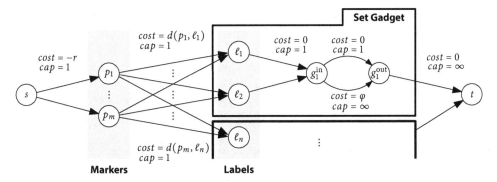

Figure 4.18: The flow network from Figure 4.3, augmented with *set gadgets* (framed in black).

gadget by directed edges E_{in}. For every edge $e \in E_{in}$, we set $cost(e) = 0$ and $cap(e) = 1$. This capacity constraint guarantees that every label fragment is matched at most once. From g_i^{in} to g_i^{out}, there are two directed edges e_{free} and $e_{penalty}$, where $cost(e_{free}) = 0$ and $cap(e_{free}) = 1$, whereas $cost(e_{penalty}) = \varphi$ and $cap(e_{penalty}) = \infty$. The exit vertex g_i^{out} is connected to sink t with a directed edges e_{out} of $cost(e_{out}) = 0$ and $cap(e_{out}) = \infty$.

Like in Section 4.3, we calculate a minimum cost flow in the constructed network. This can be done in polynomial time using standard methods, thereby solving FRAGMENT ASSIGNMENT (DISJOINT SETS). This shows that our extended optimization model, though NP-hard in general, can be solved efficiently in a realistic (restricted) case.

4.7 Concluding Remarks

In this chapter, we have considered the problem of determining the correct matching between labels and markers in historical maps. We assumed that the bounding boxes of these map elements are given. We have developed several optimization models based on such input and have given either efficient algorithms or hardness proofs for each.

We have experimentally demonstrated that the algorithm for our main model has high accuracy when run on accurate input (that is, a manually-extracted ground truth): it has error measure in the low single digits. Additionally, we have shown that it copes well with a reasonable amount of noise. We have done this by realistically perturbing the ground truth and evaluating how this influences the output of the algorithm.

In order to further improve the quality of the results, we have proposed several extensions to the original algorithm. First, we have presented a system that allows interactive postprocessing of the matches calculated by our algorithm. The system calculates a measure of confidence in the matches and presents unclear situations to a user for verification. This selection procedure performs well in identifying parts of the map that need careful human attention or even research. In addition, we have explored ways to extend our problem definition to deal with fragments of labels. While this problem is NP-hard in general, we have given an efficient algorithm for a reasonable restricted version.

Here, we have only previewed an early prototype of a user interface for our system. In future work, this could be extended to a comprehensive user interface with proper interaction design: the current user interface is very primitive from a human-computer interaction point of view, but a proper design was beyond the scope of the current work. In the context of interaction, our contribution has instead been the automatic detection of parts of the map that *need* interaction.

For an improved user interface, one could display a modern-day map next to the historical map for reference. Adding geographic context might help the user to deal with ambiguity. On the algorithmic front, future work could engage in finding a method to quickly recompute sensitivity values once the matching changes due to user feedback. This is not trivial (recall that it takes more than a minute to perform our sensitivity analysis on the *Circulus Franconicus* map from scratch), but is crucial for a real-time interactive postprocessing system. Since matching markers with label fragments is hard, the task of linking label fragments should possibly be addressed independently in a preprocessing step.

Another direction for future work is designing a user interface for the set disambiguation problem of Figure 4.17. Once a user provides information on the correct assignment of an ambiguous label fragment, this information can be propagated, possibly enabling the automatic assignment of other fragments. This should have propagation properties similar to the matching sensitivity.

Acknowledgments

We thank Hans-Günter Schmidt of the Würzburg University Library for fruitful discussion and for providing the scans used in the experiments. We thank Julian Behringer for creating the ground truth data for our experiments. Furthermore we thank Marko Chlechowitz, Julia Kauer, Andre Löffler and Florian Wisheckel for their work on the preliminary tests shown in Figure 4.16.

Chapter 5

Extracting Building Footprints

Starting in 2013, the New York Public Library (NYPL) has been running a crowdsourcing project to extract polygonal representations of the building footprints from insurance atlases of the 19th and early 20th century. As is common in crowdsourcing projects, the overall problem was decomposed into small user tasks and each task was given to multiple users. In this chapter, we discuss a problem related to one of these tasks: improving polygons that track the outline of a building footprint in a historical map. In particular, we are interested in how to integrate multiple user answers, each consisting of a polygon ostensibly describing the same footprint.

We discuss desirable properties of a "consensus polygon" representing the majority of the user answers, and arrive at an efficient algorithm. We have evaluated the algorithm on crowdsourcing data from the NYPL and observe that our algorithmic consensus polygons are correct for 96% of the footprints whereas only 85% of the (input) user polygons are correct. The basic version of the algorithm is not scale-free; we consider two variants, including a purely combinatorial one. Finally, we evaluate the geometric precision of our consensus polygons by taking the map image back into account.

5.1 Introduction

In this chapter, we deal with the extraction of map elements for which not only their location in a map, but also their individual *shape* is of interest. Map features whose particular shapes convey useful information are for example territories and forest areas (in medium-scale maps), and city districts and building footprints (in large-scale maps). One task that is of common interest in this context is vector polygon extraction. There exist tools that produce vector representations from raster images. Examples are *GDAL Polygonize*[1] for general purposes and *ArcGIS*'s "Convert Raster to Polygon" feature[2] specifically in a geographic context. Such tools require either clean and easily recognizable polygons or human intervention to assist the polygonalization algorithm (for example clicking specific areas of an image, inputting numerous parameters, manual tracing of the image and other nonautomatable processes). Historical maps rarely conform to the ideal raster image expected by those tools, since many of them have not been printed to today's quality

---

This chapter is based on joint work with Thomas C. van Dijk, Fabian Feitsch, and Mauricio Giraldo Arteaga [BvDFA16].

[1] GDAL – Geospatial Data Abstraction Library, http://www.gdal.org/
[2] ESRI ArcGIS, https://www.arcgis.com/

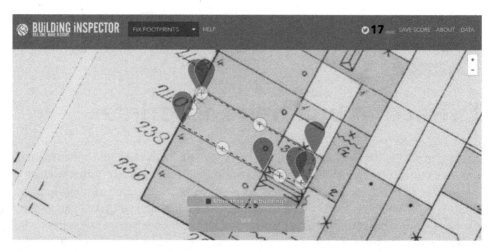

Figure 5.1: The *NYPL Building Inspector* presents a detected polygon that needs to be "fixed." Users can add, move, and delete vertices of the polygon to make it match the building footprint on the map.

standards, follow varying cartographic conventions, and are in suboptimal conservation state. Despite these challenges, it is important to efficiently and accurately extract vector representations of elements contained in these maps.

The New York Public Library has a an extensive collection of insurance atlases from the 19th and early 20th century. One of their goals is to extract polygon and attribute data from these maps [Knu13]. The collection includes tens of thousands of sheets from 1853 to 1930 organized in 200 atlases. Extracted map features are for example used in the NYPL's Space/Time Directory,[3] in which they can be linked to various related artifacts from the collections of the library.

Feature extraction was originally based on staff and volunteers, manually tracing polygons in a custom web-based GIS. Using this manual process, it took three years to extract about 179 000 polygons across three atlases. At that pace, it would be impossible to extract the bulk of the data in any reasonable amount of time. In 2013, the NYPL started development of a semi-automatic pipeline to digitize the contents of these atlases, which includes a crowdsourcing website called *Building Inspector*.[4]

As a first step in their pipeline, the scans of these maps were processed by a series of computer-vision tools in an attempt to automatically identify and extract building footprints [GA13]. This information extraction task is challenging and the extracted polygons contain a significant number of errors. The extracted polygons are then forwarded to the Building Inspector website for quality assurance and improvement in the crowd. The workflow of this system is described in Section 5.3.1; for a first impression of the user interaction, see Figure 5.1.

---

[3] http://spacetime.nypl.org/
[4] http://buildinginspector.nypl.org/

In this chapter we consider an algorithmic challenge that arises in analyzing the Building Inspector data. We call it the *polygon consensus* problem and it is informally stated as follows: given a set of polygons that are supposed to represent the same object, compute a single polygon that represents the majority opinion. We propose an algorithm for this problem and show by experimental evaluation on approximately 3000 polygons (corresponding to 200 footprints) that the computed consensus polygons have higher quality than the incoming "raw" polygons from the crowd: an improvement from 85% correct to 96% correct. Extrapolating this to all 200 atlases, this improvement represents in the order of a hundred thousand additional correct footprints – though not all atlases have been digitized yet. We also show that the computed polygons more precisely align to the image in a geometric sense.

Some parts of this chapter rely on specifics of the Building Inspector project, but the techniques and concepts are more generally applicable. For one, the project demonstrates the potential of "smart" crowdsourcing where nontrivial algorithms are applied to improve the quality of crowdsourced data; we elaborate on this in the concluding remarks. Secondly, the polygon consensus problem as such may be of independent interest to the computational geometry and GIS communities, possibly with different applications or different formalizations as an optimization problem.

5.2 Related Work

Particularly related to the current chapter is the work of Squire et al. [SRGL00]. They integrate data from multiple participants reporting on the spatial extent of an environmental contamination. In this context, they use the term consensus polygon and arrive at a definition different from ours. Much of the difference stems from the application, where theirs is most concerned with the area covered by the input polygons rather than with the shape. As a result, using their approach on the Building Inspector data would not give satisfying results. A shared ingredient is using the mean of the centroids of the input polygons (see Section 5.3.4), though it serves an entirely different purpose in their algorithm.

Volunteered Geographic Information. Crowdsourcing for geographic information is not a new concept, and under the term *volunteered geographic information* (VGI) represents an expansive field of work, with the successful OpenStreetMap project [HW08] as its poster child. See for example Goodchild [Goo07] for a general review of the concept, placing it within a context of more traditional citizen science and the role of the general public in geographic observation. For a comprehensive overview of VGI as geographic information science, see the book on the topic edited by Arsarjani et al. [AZMH15].

An important theme in VGI is data quality, in particular the quality of *volunteered* information as compared to *authoritative* information. An interesting case arises when no authoritative data is available. (This is the case in the current project: this is precisely why volunteered information was gathered.) Even in the absence of such a "ground truth", there can be many grounds for determining the reliability of information. Vandercasteele and Devillers [VD15] distinguish three aspects that one might take into consideration. The *data-centric approach* considers the operations that have been performed on a feature of the data, such as the number of committed edits. In OpenStreetMap, this correlates well with data quality [Hak10]. A *user-centric approach*, instead, considers who provides the data, and how these users relate to each other. This leads to a concept of "user quality," which can often be linked to the quality of the features, and in aggregate gives rise to *crowd quality* [vEDF10]. Lastly, the *context-centric approach* looks to the actual features of the data and how they semantically relate to each other. The current work can be seen in this context, though instead of using semantic relations between *different* objects, we use the geometric relations between several user-provided representation of the *same* object. (Future work could address the semantic relations between the submitted footprints of different buildings as well, for example by clustering them.)

Map Conflation. In terms of dealing with multiple representations of the same spatial data, our problem can also be considered a *map conflation* problem. Longley et al. [LGMR15] define map conflation as the attempt to "replace two or more versions of the same information with a single version that reflects the pooling [...] of the sources." Note that unlike in the common map conflation setting (where relatively few, feature-rich maps are merged), we have a potentially large number of representations of the same, relatively simple spatial object (a building footprint).

Extracting Vector Data. Extracting (vector) features from raster map images, including scanned historical maps, is an active field of research. Chiang et al. [CLK14] present a comprehensive survey on digital map processing techniques. The building footprints used for the experiments in this chapter were extracted with an image processing pipeline by Giraldo Arteaga [GA13]. There are multiple other approaches for extracting building footprints, such as those by Laycock et al. [LBLD11], Liu [Liu02] and Miyoshi et al. [MLK+04]. These approaches do not solve the problem reliably and do not obviate the need for our crowdsourcing step. Indeed, their polygons could be used as input for a crowdsourcing project.

There is also research on the extraction of other features from raster maps, such as city quarters extracted from historical cadastral maps by Raveaux et al. [RBO08]. Extracting road vector data is a particularly popular topic (for example [CK13b, HL09, BAU07]). Marciano et al. [MAHL13] extract (polygonal) city districts from historical city maps in a largely manual process using on ArcGIS. In order to find archaeologically interesting sites, White [Whi13] manually traces and annotates polygonal features in historical city maps of New Orleans. Leyk et al. [LBW06] describe a method to find forest cover in a set of 19th century topographic maps. More general approaches for the segmentation of color layers are also described by Leyk [Ley10].

Computational Geometry. In the context of computational geometry, there is some research on "consensus" among geometric objects. This includes for example median trajectories [vKW11, BBvK+13], which have the property that all points are supported by at least one of the input trajectories. To handle inaccurate input trajectories, De La Cruz et al. [DLCKP+14] introduce mean consensus trajectories. These algorithms have no direct bearing on our building footprint problem: they have a problem we will discuss in some detail in Section 5.3.2.

The algorithm presented in this chapter is based on a heuristic currently employed by the NYPL to deal with their polygon consensus problem in practice. The description of their algorithm is only available online[5]; we will describe all relevant details in Section 5.3.

5.3 Polygon Consensus

In this section we discuss the polygon consensus problem. First, we describe the setup of the crowdsourcing project that gave rise to the data set being considered. Then we discuss what properties we might want from a consensus polygon. Finally we describe our proposed algorithm and two variants.

5.3.1 User Tasks

This chapter is based on data from a two-stage crowdsourcing project. Its web-based software supports various annotation tasks on scans of the maps in the system. Before the crowd gets involved, a pipeline of image processing tools is used to extract polygons from the map image [GA13]. The set of extracted polygons unfortunately contains many errors; this computer vision problem cannot be considered solved. In the first task in the crowd workflow, the user is shown an automatically detected polygon overlaid on the map image and has to make the following decision.

> "You are inspecting a polygon to find out if its shape: matches a building (value: YES), matches part of a building but needs fixing (value: FIX) or does not match a building at all (value: NO)."

A screenshot of the user interface is presented in Figure 5.2. Polygons for which a major-ity of at least three users vote YES are assumed to be correct. In case of majority NO the polygon is discarded as a useless failure of the image processing step. In this chapter we focus on the interesting (third) case of FIX polygons.[6] These are processed in a second crowdsourcing task, where users are shown such a polygon and are instructed to make it match the underlying building footprint by adding, deleting and moving vertices (see Figure 5.1).

---

[5] http://nbviewer.jupyter.org/gist/mgiraldo/a68b53175ce5892531bc
[6] Approximately 13% of the detected polygons fall into this category.

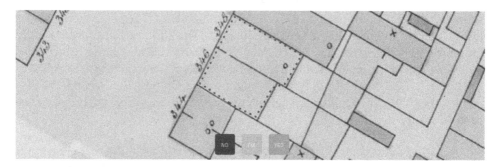

Figure 5.2: The user interface for the first task in the crowdsourcing workflow: deciding whether an automatically extracted building footprint is correct, to be fixed, or completely incorrect. In the case of the building footprint highlighted in this screenshot, the crowd user should answer "fix", since the polygon covers two separate buildings but is not entirely wrong.

As we will see in Section 5.4, only about 85% of the "fixed" polygons we get from the crowd are indeed correct. In order to increase reliability, multiple independent users are given the same polygon to fix. Hence as an answer from the crowd we obtain, for every automatically detect polygon, a set of polygons created by different users that are each supposed to be a fixed version of the detected polygon. We call this a *group* of polygons, and its elements *user polygons*. By the nature of the interface and the problem, all of these polygons will differ: at least slightly in the exact position of manually-edited vertices, and possibly in the user's judgment of how to fix the polygon. This leads to the problem addressed in this chapter: given a set of user-created polygons, how can we find one *consensus* polygon that represents best what the majority of the users intended?[7]

5.3.2 Modeling

We start with two general considerations about the properties a "consensus polygon" should have; these are deliberately vague at this point.

- If the input group consists of many similarly-shaped polygons, but possibly includes some amount of outlier polygons of a different shape, then a consensus polygon should be shaped similarly to the majority of the polygons.

- If a set of vertices from different polygons are near each other and, structurally within their polygon, serve a similar function, then a consensus polygon should consider these as noisy representations of an actual vertex. Such a set of vertices should result in a *single* vertex of a consensus polygon. An alternate view of this consideration is that the consensus polygon should have a level of detail that is similar to the (majority of the) input polygons.

---

[7] It would be possible to feed this consensus polygon (or the fixed polygons) back into the first step of the Building Inspector to see if they are correct; we have not evaluated this, but discuss the idea in our concluding remarks. Here, we are interested in evaluating the quality of the consensus step itself.

We do not give a formal definition of polygon consensus as an optimization problem; this is an interesting avenue for future work, particularly because the appropriate definition of consensus may depend on the application and spelling out explicit optimization criteria and constraints is good practice. At present, we give a reasonable heuristic algorithm and show that it gives good results on the Building Inspector data. This NYPL-developed algorithm was previously only described online; we describe it here with some minor improvements and clarifications as compared to the version available online.

We conclude this section with a discussion of alternate approaches and their short-comings. A natural and elegantly simple attempt at defining a consensus polygon is to consider the intersection or the union of the polygons in a group. More generally, we could take the polygon formed by the set of points where at least k polygons overlap. This effectively corresponds to taking a vote for all points in the plane independently. Conceptually, this algorithm is concerned with the interior of polygons and, at least for our problem, that is not the right view: it is too local, and we care more about vertices – that is, corners of buildings. In other words, the combinatorial shape and structure of the polygon is more important to us than exact coverage. Indeed, we will see in Section 5.4.4 that the real problem we face is semantic correctness, and geometric precision follows from that. For our application, the main problem with the intersection-based approach is that it is likely to give a consensus polygon with many more vertices than the input polygons, many of them close together, which is counter to the second desideratum. The median trajectories discussed in Section 5.2 suffer from the same problem. It might be possible to get rid of these spurious vertices in a postprocessing step, for example using a simplification algorithm, but this takes away from the elegant simplicity of the algo-rithm. Incidentally, this intersection-based approach might actually be well suited for Squire et al.'s contamination data [SRGL00].

5.3.3 Vertex Voting

The basic vertex voting algorithm takes a set of polygons as input and computes a con-sensus polygon (or decides that there is no consensus): first it clusters the vertices of the input polygons and then finds a cycle through the clusters that is supported by many of the input polygons.

The algorithm starts by determining a set of candidate vertices for the consensus poly-gon. For this purpose, it takes the set of all vertices from the input polygons and clusters it using DBSCAN. It requires, as a parameter, the distance threshold ε for points to be considered "near." We set its other parameter, the minimum number of points $minPts$ required to form a cluster, to 1 unless otherwise noted. Note that this makes it effectively single-linkage clustering [SSBD14], since two points with a distance less than ε suffice to form a nontrivial cluster (of size 2). Later we will discuss a situation in which we use higher values for $minPts$ to effectively identify noise.

Let C be the set of clusters determined by the clustering algorithm. Each cluster $C \in C$ consists of a set of input vertices and represents a candidate vertex of the consensus poly-gon. In the second step, the algorithm searches for a cycle through the clusters, which will define the edges of the consensus polygon. This cycle is heuristically constructed in the following way, after picking a consistent orientation of the polygons.

Let (u, v) be any arc in an input polygon, and let C be the cluster that v is in: then we say that u *votes* for C. The algorithm starts in an arbitrary cluster containing the most vertices, then it iteratively proceeds to the cluster that has the most votes among the vertices in the current cluster (breaking ties arbitrarily). This process is terminated when a cluster is visited for the second time, and the resulting cycle of clusters is taken as the combinatorial structure of the consensus polygon. Note that we may return to a different cluster than the first. If the resulting cycle contains at least three clusters, we construct the consensus polygon by connecting the centroid of each cluster along the cycle. Otherwise, the algorithm does not output a consensus polygon.

Theorem 5.1. *Let $\mathcal{P}$ be a set of polygons with a total of n vertices, and let C be a clustering of these vertices. The basic vertex voting algorithm runs in $O(n)$ time.*

Proof. We assume that we can enumerate the points in a cluster. The basic vertex voting algorithm first identifies a largest cluster in C; this takes $O(n)$ time. Beginning at that cluster, the algorithm tallies the votes from all points in the cluster and proceeds to the cluster that received the most votes. Once a cluster is visited for the second time, this process is stopped. This guarantees that each point is tallied at most once, resulting in a runtime of $O(n)$.

Finally, the algorithm calculates the centroids of each cluster in the resulting cycle (if it contains at least three clusters), which again takes $O(n)$ time in total. If the cycle contains less than three clusters, this step is omitted and the algorithm returns nothing. The voting algorithm thus runs in $O(n)$ time. □

Next, we consider the runtime of the clustering step. Let n again be the number of vertices in all input polygons combined. Without a data structure to speed up region queries, the runtime of DBSCAN is $\Theta(n^2)$. The generally accepted observation that a runtime of $O(n \log n)$ can be expected in many cases when using appropriate spatial data structures [EKSX96] does not necessarily hold for our data. Assume a fixed building footprint and let the number of polygons in the group go to infinity. Then if at least a constant fraction of the polygons contribute a vertex to at least a constant fraction of the clusters, each individual region query is likely to return $\Omega(n)$ vertices. The runtime of clustering dominates that of tallying the votes and performing the graph search, leading to a total runtime of $O(n^2)$.

We note that the voting algorithm is sensitive to the winding of the input polygons: reversing the orientation of all polygons and running the voting algorithm is not guaranteed to give the reverse consensus polygon (see Figure 5.3). Being independent of the winding would be a desirable property of a consensus algorithm, but the example for our algorithm can be considered pathological – indeed, in our data set we have encountered no such group.

Some groups may contain extreme outliers, that is, polygons that have been entered erroneously and do not describe the semantically correct shape at all. We observe ex-

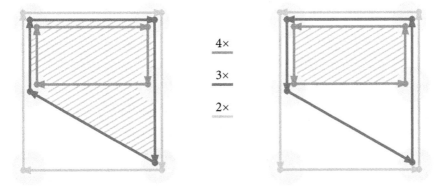

Figure 5.3: Instance in which the orientation of the input polygons affects the resulting consensus polygon. The input consists of multiple copies of the three depicted polygons; the consensus polygon is indicated by the light blue stripes.

perimentally that the voting algorithm is somewhat robust in the presence of this kind of noise (see Section 5.4). If the input groups contain a large number of spurious polygons, it might be necessary to filter them beforehand. In the next section, we present a variation of the Voting algorithm that includes such a preprocessing step (at the cost of introducing an additional parameter).

It is unfortunate that the parameter ε makes the algorithm scale dependent. Depending on the application, it is to pick a reasonable value of ε, as this parameter reflects a rather direct property of the input data: the amount of "noise" we expect on vertices of the input polygons. For cases where the scale of the input polygons is unknown or varies by group, having a single fixed ε is problematic. In Section 5.3.5, we present a variation of the algorithm that is scale-free and indeed parameter-free.

5.3.4 Filtering

Assume that an input group contains outliers (see for example Figure 5.4). This can lead to errors when using the basic vertex voting algorithm. We alleviate this problem by adding a filtering step before the clustering. For each polygon in the group, we consider the centroid of its vertices. If these centroids are far apart, it is unlikely that their polygons describe the same shape (building footprint). Hence we cluster the centroids: we use DBSCAN with another distance threshold φ. If this results in more than one cluster, all polygons not in the largest cluster are discarded before running the voting algorithm.

Unfortunately, the parameter φ does not have a clean interpretation in the application domain and is less intuitive than ε. Still, this variant of the algorithm is currently used in production in the Building Inspector, where it slightly improves the performance of the system (see Section 5.4).

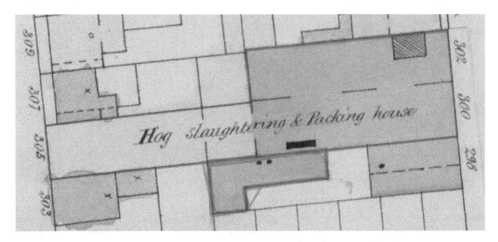

Figure 5.4: The polygons in this group describe two different buildings. There is a single polygon representing the footprint of the *Hog slaughtering & Packing house* on top, and 50 polygons describing the L-shaped building below (of which one is noticeably imprecise).

5.3.5 Scale-Free Voting

Next we present a parameter-free version of the voting algorithm, which we call Auto-ε. Various general-purpose attempts have been made to get rid of the parameters in DB-SCAN, such as with the OPTICS algorithm [ABKS99]. We take a more direct approach to finding an appropriate value for ε by focusing on a domain aspect of our application: the number of corners of the building. The intuition is that most users will give us a polygon with the right number of vertices: we pick ε such that we get that number of clusters. (Note that we still profit from using DBSCAN as opposed to, for example, the k-means algorithm: we can use the density constraints to remove noise.)

Consider what happens when DBSCAN is run with varying values of ε. We set its *minPts* parameter to $\lceil k/2 \rceil$, where k is the number of polygons in the group; fixing this particular value of *minPts* ensures that each cluster is supported by a majority of the input polygons. Now note that, given the polygons, the number of clusters is solely a function of ε. Call this function f and note that it is not bitonic (as one might expect): it can increase and decrease repeatedly, since increasing ε can cause clusters to merge but can also result in the creation of new clusters due to the density condition. See Figure 5.5 for an example of the behavior of f on a real group from our data set. This diagram is somewhat related in motivation to the *k-distance graph* that the authors of the original DBSCAN paper propose for parameter selection, but it is in fact quite distinct and more amenable to automatic analysis.

Let m be the median number of vertices in a polygon in the group. We consider a value of ε to be plausible only if $f(\varepsilon) = m$; it remains to find and pick one such value. There may be multiple intervals of plausible values of ε. In that case, we take a value from the largest interval: in this interval, getting the right number of clusters is most

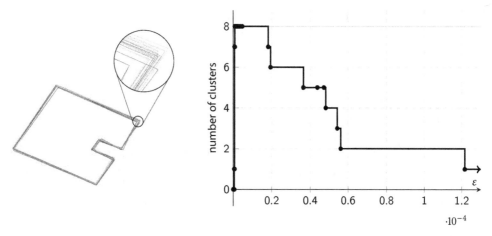

Figure 5.5: *Left:* a group of polygons from our data set. *Right:* a diagram showing the number of clusters for different values of ε for that group. Note that the desired number of eight clusters is reached quickly and remains stable for some time. The next stable plateau is reached when the clusters on the inside merge together. Because the outline is nearly a square, there is a long plateau with two clusters before collapsing into one cluster.

stable to small changes in ε, which is a property we expect of the correct clustering. In the diagram in Figure 5.5, this corresponds to the longest plateau at the correct height.

The Auto-ε consensus polygon is given by running the voting algorithm (without filtering) using this ε. It would be possible to combine Auto-ε and the filtering from Section 5.3.4, but then we reintroduce φ and have a scale dependent algorithm; we do not consider this a reasonable variant and do not evaluate it.

For the runtime of computing the Auto-ε consensus polygon, consider the following theorem.

Theorem 5.2. *The distinct results of the DBSCAN algorithm over all ε can be enumerated in $O(n^2 \log n)$ time, where n is the number of points and $minPts$ is fixed.*

Proof. Recall that a core point is defined as having at least $minPts$ points within its ε-neighborhood. As ε increases, points can become core points and clusters can merge. While the algorithm sweeps over increasing values of ε, we store at each point a list of all other points within distance ε: call this the neighbor list. We furthermore store the core points in a disjoint-set data structure [CLRS09] to keep track of the clusters.

We consider the DBSCAN results for increasing ε. With $\varepsilon = 0$, only multiply occurring identical points can form clusters, and they do so when their multiplicity is at least $minPts$. This initializes the neighbor lists and the clusters. Nothing changes until ε equals the shortest nonzero distance between two points. Consider this pair of points: each gains a neighbor within distance ε, which is added to their neighbor lists and may cause them to become core points. Whenever a point becomes a core point, we make a set for it in the disjoint-set data structure and immediately union this set with the sets of all points in its neighbor list. The sets in the data structure represent the clusters in the DBSCAN result for this value of ε. We repeat this process for every pair of points in increasing order of distance.

For the claimed runtime, create a list of all $O(n^2)$ pairs of input points and sort it by increasing distance in $O(n^2 \log n)$ time. Handle the pairs of points in this order. Every point becomes a core point once, which directly leads to a MAKE-SET call. Its newly-made set must also be merged with all its neighboring core points. These are available in the neighbor list and we observe that every pair of points is considered only twice: when either of the vertices becomes a core point. With an efficient disjoint-set data structure [Tar75, CLRS09], this costs amortized $O(\alpha(n))$ time for a FIND-SET and possibly a UNION operation, where α is the inverse Ackermann function. This leads to a total runtime of $O(n^2 \cdot \alpha(n))$ for keeping track of the clusters. This is dominated by the initial sorting step. □

It follows that we can compute the Auto-ε consensus polygon in $O(n^2 \log n)$ time, since we can also keep track of the number of clusters during the above algorithm and use that to determine ε; the cost of the other steps is lower.

As an example, consider Figure 5.5. For $\varepsilon = 0$, no clusters are formed. Increasing ε initially leads to an increase in the number of clusters: in a quick succession of events, ε becomes large enough to cover at least half of the vertices in the various corners of the shape. Then, nothing changes for a while. There are several plateaus in which the number of clusters does not change for an interval of values of ε. In particular, the plot shows a plateau at value eight and this is the number we are looking for. For higher values of ε, the clusters collapse and ultimately become a single cluster; increasing ε beyond this value has no further effects.

5.4 Experiments

We have implemented the three variants of our algorithm and evaluated their performance on data from the Building Inspector project, which is publicly available through an open API.[8] At the time of our experiments, the data set consisted of 5834 groups that have been labeled FIX, containing 58 651 user polygons. We have sampled a random subset of 200 groups for the experiments presented in this chapter, where we have restricted the sample to groups containing at most 9 polygons.[9] We have run the three variants of our algorithm successfully on all 200 groups, resulting in 600 algorithmic consensus polygons. Together with the corresponding 1278 user polygons and the 200 polygons detected by the computer vision step, this makes a total of 2078 polygons assessed in this section.

---

[8] `http://buildinginspector.nypl.org/data`
[9] We only consider groups with at most 9 user polygons to avoid some rare groups that contain very many user polygons (up to 70). This restriction allows us to manually inspect groups without inordinate effort and should not significantly influence the results.

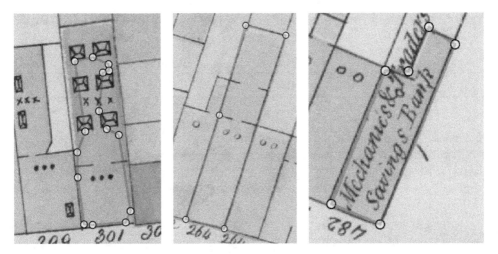

Figure 5.6: The polygon on the left is semantically incorrect because it does not represent a building footprint. The polygon in the middle is also incorrect, because it has one vertex too many. The polygon on the right has inaccurate corner positions, but is semantically correct because it covers the right shape and has exactly one vertex for each corner.

5.4.1 What Is Consensus?

In our first set of experiments, we manually evaluated the consensus polygons in terms of their *semantic* correctness. This means that we checked for each polygon whether it actually traces a building footprint on the map. (We will explain our criteria for that in more detail below.) Note that this manual evaluation only addresses the semantic correctness of each individual polygon – in particular, it does not take into account *which* building footprint a given polygon resembles, or if that footprint represents a reasonable consensus for the group. This avoids the need for a definition of polygon consensus: all user polygons are supposed to trace the same object, so the fact that an output polygon is a correct polygon can reasonably be taken as proxy for it being an appropriate consensus.

Note that this measure is thwarted by an algorithm that always returns *some* semantically correct polygon that is unrelated to the input, but clearly all our computed polygons are appropriately related to the input group.

5.4.2 Ground Truth

We have manually created a ground truth in terms of semantic correctness as follows. We call a polygon correct if it traces a single building footprint and has exactly one vertex for each corner of the footprint (and no vertices where there are no corners). Examples of polygons that are semantically correct or incorrect according to these criteria are presented in Figure 5.6. Three referees[10] independently evaluated the correctness of all 2078

---

[10] Thomas C. van Dijk, Fabian Feitsch, and the author.

Table 5.1: Ratio of correct polygons among the detected polygons to be fixed, the user polygons, and the algorithmic consensus polygons.

set of polygons	FIX	User	VotingPre	VotingRaw	Auto-ε
ratio of correct polygons	0.0	0.847	0.96	0.94	0.705

polygons by manual inspection. To avoid influencing this judgment, all polygons were randomly shuffled and it was unclear to the referees which came from which source. In our experience, only the FIX polygons are identifiable as such.[11] For polygons with conflicting votes among the three referees (which was the case with 84 polygons), the majority answer was taken.

Some groups in our data set contained outliers as discussed in Section 5.3.4, that is, user polygons tracing more than one building. We call a group *divisive* if its polygons trace at least two disjoint objects (for an example, see Figure 5.4). Approximately 20% of the 200 groups in our sample are divisive. Such groups occur because the crowdsourced user task is somewhat underspecified: starting with a polygon that needs to be fixed, there is sometimes uncertainty as to what building footprint is supposed to be traced. (For an example of such a situation, look back to Figure 5.2: should the user trace building no. 346 or 348?). At the time of our evaluation, the crowdsourcing was already running for three years, which made changes to the user task undesirable. The lesson learned for future applications, is to make sure that user tasks have a uniquely-defined solution: in this case, making sure that users agree on which object to trace. If the user task is underspecified, as in our experiment, one needs to be prepared to handle the divergent user answers algorithmically afterward (which may well be possible). As we will see in the outcomes of our experiments, divisive groups had a particularly strong impact on the Auto-ε algorithm.

5.4.3 Semantic Correctness

Next we discuss the outcomes of the semantic evaluation; Table 5.1 provides statistics. Of the 200 polygons that were detected through computer vision, we found that none are semantically correct. This is no surprise since they have been marked as FIX in the first crowdsourcing step. Still, this confirms that our criteria for semantic correctness are consistent with the task as interpreted by the crowd. The user polygons have a high semantic correctness (average 84.7%). On 129 of the 200 footprints, the users were able to solve the problem consistently: more than 80% of the user polygons in each of these groups were correct. The remaining groups raised more difficulties; for 15 of them, at least half of the user polygons were semantically incorrect (see Figure 5.7).

---

[11] Consider for example the left polygon in Figure 5.6. It is quite obvious that this polygon was not submitted by a user, but is the result of an error during the automatic detection. For the other two polygons, the source is not apparent.

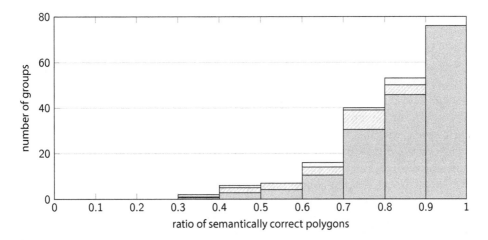

Figure 5.7: This histogram shows groups binned by the ratio of semantically correct user polygons within the group. The dark gray portion of each bar indicates the expected number of correct groups using the baseline algorithm. The striped portion on top gives the additional number of correct groups when running VotingPre instead. Groups that remain incorrect for both algorithms are indicated in light gray. Note that the striped portion of each bar reflects the gain of our algorithm.

Table 5.2: Average ratio of correct user polygons per group, binned by the number of user polygons in the group.

number of polygons in group	3	4	5	6	7	8	9
ratio of correct user polygons	0.67	0.88	0.85	0.86	0.89	0.81	0.80
support		2	6	7	16	40	53	76

Not all groups have the same number of user polygons; this did not significantly influence the ratio of semantically correct polygons (see Table 5.2). This supports our assumption that the users' polygons are indeed independent, with a certain probability of errors. We consider an accuracy of 84.7% to be a reasonable quality level for individual tasks in a crowdsourcing project. It certainly gives the hope that integrating multiple user answers for the same footprint can be used to increase the success rate by taking some kind of majority vote.

In the following, we consider a consensus polygon *successful* if it is semantically correct; based on this, we calculate the *success rate* of the three variants of our algorithm. In addition, we consider the randomized algorithm that takes a random user polygon from the group as a baseline. This could be considered "consensus" in the sense that if many polygons agree, one of those is likely to be picked. In expectation, this algorithm has a success rate of 85.2% on our data. Note that this number is different from the 84.7% reported above; this is because the baseline algorithm picks exactly one polygon from each *group*, whereas the number above is an average over all polygons.

We now consider the voting algorithm with filtering (called VotingPre in the data). It is successful on 96% of the groups. This can be considered a success for the whole project: the 11.3 percentage point increase in accuracy over the user polygons represents more than 6600 additional correct footprints when extrapolated to the full data set. This calculation assumes as baseline the algorithm discussed above: pick a random user polygon from a group and return it as the consensus. Figure 5.7 presents the gain in correct polygons for the 200 groups in our experiment.

However, recall that this variant of the algorithm requires two parameters, which can be problematic depending on the data set to be processed. Next we consider the voting algorithm without filtering (called VotingRaw in the data), which has one parameter fewer due to the lack of the filtering step. As a result of this, the accuracy takes a small hit, dropping from 96% to 94%. This is still well above the users' base rate of 84.7%. We note that VotingPre does not actually dominate VotingRaw: seven groups were correct only for VotingPre, three only for VotingRaw.

In these first two experiments, we have set ε (and also φ in the case of VotingPre) to effective values by hand. The experiments have shown that we can remove the filtering step at only a minor cost. This leaves ε, for which a reasonable value can be picked in many cases, based by manual inspection of the map images and the user polygons. However, even with a carefully picked value of ε some problems remain when a footprint contains very short edges; for an example, look ahead at Figure 5.9 (left). Also, due to their dependence on the parameters ε and φ, both these variants of the algorithm are not scale-free. A failure mode of the variants with fixed parameter ε is indeed when the vertex clustering (using DBSCAN) fails.

Next, we discuss the performance of the Auto-ε algorithm. It has a much lower success rate than the previous variants, at 70.5%. This is even lower than the base rate for user polygons. This may sound unacceptable, but is caused by a very specific type of errors that our users make: disagreeing on which object to trace, resulting in divisive groups. If there is significant disagreement in this sense, the Auto-ε algorithm will not be able to find a reasonable value for ε that yields the required number of clusters. This leads to a set of candidate vertices that do not correspond well with the corners of the footprints, which prevents the algorithm from finding a semantically correct consensus polygon. For an example of this, see Figure 5.8. Note that the clusters for the variants with fixed ε are not affected by this problem: these algorithms are still able to return *some* semantically correct polygon.

Manually inspecting the incorrect consensus polygons returned by the Auto-ε algorithm, we see that 42 out of 45 groups are indeed divisive. With an effective filtering step for such groups, the Auto-ε algorithm would reach an error rate at least as good as those of the two other variants (on our data set). We could do the filtering from Section 5.3.4, but that reintroduces the parameter φ – which defeats most of the purpose of the Auto-ε algorithm. We have therefore ignored this possibility.

We do note Auto-ε is the sole correct algorithm for two groups (1%) where our fixed ε fails (see Figure 5.9). Note that this is relatively rare on *our* data, but could be more common in other applications where the traced objects are less uniform in scale: consider

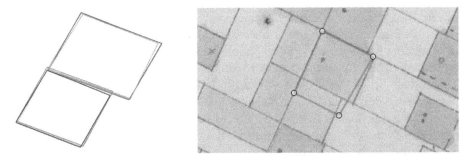

Figure 5.8: Situation in which Auto-ε fails. All polygons in the group have four corners, but mark two different footprints (left). The Auto-ε algorithm picks the longest plateau with four clusters, which can only be reached when corners merge, resulting in an incorrect consensus polygon (right).

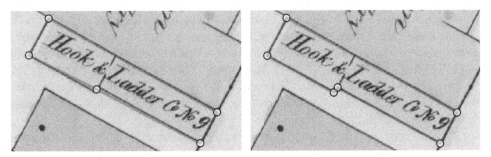

Figure 5.9: Situation in which using a constant ε value leads to an error. VotingPre cannot detect the small detail in the center, because the corners have been assigned to the same cluster (left). In contrast, Auto-ε is able to adjust the clustering accordingly and finds the correct solution (right).

for example a data set that includes polygons describing cities and countries, where different values for ε are required for handling different groups. Clustering algorithm such as OPTICS [ABKS99] might able to handle this, but we have the additional structure of groups, and the Auto-ε algorithm is able to pick an appropriate ε for each one.

Our experiments show that we can get rid of one parameter (by removing the filtering, if we have a good ε) or both (by automatically determining ε). However, the latter option only works if we have a good way to filter the data. In practice, one can select one of the three variants of our algorithm depending on the particular data set to be processed.

5.4.4 Geometric Precision

In the previous experiments, the correctness of the polygons was determined manually and in terms of semantics. We now evaluate the *geometric* precision of the polygons by taking the map images back into account. This closes the circle in some sense, since the polygons have been extracted from the images using computer vision at the beginning of the pipeline.

For the evaluation of geometric precision, we consider the brightness of the pixels under the edges of the polygon: if the edges indeed follow the ink marking the outline of a building footprint, these pixels should be relatively dark. This is opposed to the relatively bright color of the (blank) paper and the background colors used to fill the building footprints.[12] We use a standard brightness calculation[13] and normalize to a scale where black is 0 and white is 1. Note that this approach works as a measure of fit, but not for extracting the polygons without further information: we will show below that we cannot distinguish correct polygons from incorrect ones based on their brightness.

Considering the average brightness scores (see Figure 5.10), we see that the polygons detected by computer vision (and marked as FIX) have an average brightness of 0.68, which we will see is high. This means that these polygons do not align well with the underlying building footprints on the maps, because a significant fraction of their edges runs over blank paper rather than inked lines. The semantically correct user polygons have a much better score (0.49), which suggests that assessing the brightness is actually is a sensible measure of success. However, the semantically incorrect user polygons have a similar score (0.54): this already hints at the fact that a brightness analysis alone will not solve semantics. Indeed, in 15 of the 200 groups in our data set, the polygon with the best brightness score is semantically incorrect: this is only slightly better than the base rate. An example showing correct and incorrect polygons together with their brightness scores is presented in Figure 5.11.

Statistics confirm that the brightness score cannot individually be considered a good feature for determining the semantic correctness of a polygon. Consider a classifier that, given a discrimination threshold τ, assumes that all polygons with brightness lower than τ are correct. The quality of this classifier can be evaluated using a receiver operating characteristic (ROC) curve. We calculated the ROC curve using our ground truth data (Figure 5.12); the area under curve (AUC) is 0.643. Generally, an AUC value between 0.5 and 0.7 is considered "poor discrimination, not much better than a coin toss" [HJL04]. This shows that the correctness of a polygon can not reasonably be judged by its brightness alone.

The score of the consensus polygons calculated by the three variants of our algorithm is each better than the average score of USER polygons (0.440 for the correct polygons, see Figure 5.10). This is mainly because the algorithms take the centroid of each vertex cluster, thus evening out inaccurately placed input vertices. This evaluation shows that the consensus polygons outperform the users' base rate not only in terms of semantic correctness, but also in geometric precision.

We conclude this section with an outlook to possible improvements based on assessing the geometric precision. In order to obtain polygons with precision even higher than that of the polygons returned by our algorithms, we could use the brightness score for

---

[12] While the background colors certainly contain interesting information, it is not straightforward to use these colors for extracting building footprints from our maps: they have degraded over time, making it difficult to distinguish them from each other and the background [GA13].

[13] We define the brightness of a pixel as the mean of the largest and smallest value of the RGB channels, normalized to a value between 0 and 1.

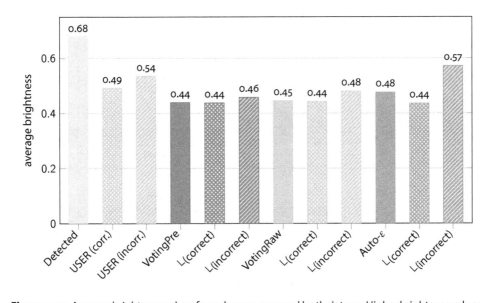

Figure 5.10: Average brightness values for polygons, grouped by their type. Higher brightness values mean less precision in terms of the underlying building footprint.

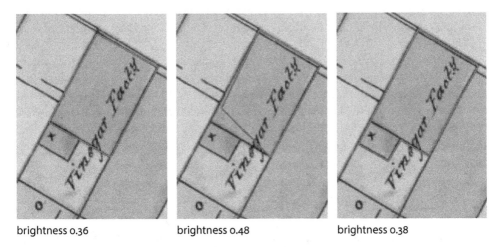

brightness 0.36   brightness 0.48   brightness 0.38

Figure 5.11: The polygon on the left has low average brightness and is semantically correct. The polygon in the center has a worse brightness, but we also consider it to be correct. The polygon on the right has a better brightness, but is semantically incorrect as it marks the union of two footprints.

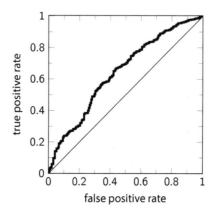

Figure 5.12: ROC curve for thresholding user polygons by brightness. The area under curve is 0.643, indicating poor classification performance.

a local search algorithm starting from a consensus polygon. Such an algorithm could for example repeatedly slightly move the vertices of a polygon and re-evaluate the brightness score after each move. If the score improves, the new position is kept for the next iteration; otherwise, the vertex is returned to its previous position.

Applying local search is dangerous: there is no guarantee that the resulting polygon with locally minimal brightness is semantically correct. Still, if we start the local search on a polygon that is close to a semantically correct footprint (and carefully restrict the moving distance), we may expect it to converge to a higher-precision version without introducing semantic mistakes. Whereas many advanced local search algorithms are designed to *escape* local optima, we may actually be better served by a straightforward greedy approach.

We think the above could be an interesting general approach for human computation [LvA11]: local search to a high-precision solution, supported by a user to get it into the basin of attraction of the semantically correct solution. In the case of polygon consensus, this may improve the geometric accuracy of the results, but recall that only 85% of user polygons were semantically correct, so this does not invalidate the consensus step. A video of our preliminary experiments with the approach sketched above can be found online.[14]

5.5 Concluding Remarks

The present chapter considers a data set gathered in a specific crowdsourcing project at the New York Public Library. Algorithmic analysis of this data results in higher-quality output, increasing the value of the gathered data. We propose the general usefulness of such *smart crowdsourcing*, where the user task is not simply a multiple-choice question,

---

[14] https://www.youtube.com/watch?v=GOzlprNa22o

and where the integration of the responses may be nontrivial. This will be particularly important for the development of successful crowdsourcing projects for (historical) spatial information, since such information can be hard to capture in discrete, multiple-choice questions. In OpenStreetMap [HW08], a classic example of a system gathering information provided by volunteers, eventual correctness comes (at a most basic level) from a community effort of correcting errors and moderating changes. This is a rather "brute force" application of user effort and we wonder about the possible gains in efficiency achievable when an efficient user task is designed in tandem with appropriate algorithms (compare with human computation [LvA11]).

The algorithms and techniques in this chapter are generally applicable, though the image processing to extract the initial polygons was bespoke and might not readily generalize to other maps. When applying the consensus algorithms to other data sets, a variant should be chosen based on the types of errors that are expected in the input as discussed at the end of Section 5.4.3.

We have also mentioned the possibility to feed a consensus polygon (or a user-fixed polygon) back into the first step of the presented crowdsourcing process. This has the advantage that the crowd users can directly judge those polygons, and potentially also fix errors in them. The downsides of such an approach include that the user-submitted content is no longer separated from other users – this can be problematic, for example when users submit obscenities.

The map sheets in the Building Inspector project have already been georectified as part of their digitization, prior to our involvement. The extraction of individual features (here: building footprints) is a clear example of deep georeferencing, where we do not just have the map image in a known coordinate system, but also know about the object-level semantic elements on the map. This enables rich data experiences such as the NYPL's Space/Time Directory[15] and virtual reality applications [BGG+16].

We have introduced the idea of using local search as postprocessing for our consensus polygons, but as noted, this only works as a postprocessing step: it cannot solve the question of whether a polygon is semantically correct or not. The concept of using a myopic local search to get to a local optimum, with user input to get into the correct basin of attraction seems like it might be of more general interest.

Acknowledgments

We thank Mauricio Giraldo Arteaga of the New York Public Library for the enjoyable and fruitful cooperation.

---

[15] http://spacetime.nypl.org/

Chapter 6

Georeferencing Historical Itineraries

In this chapter, we present a system that extracts spatial information from textual representations given in historical itineraries. Many historical itineraries describe routes by listing settlements (and travel distances) along the way. In order to automatically extract information from these documents, we develop an approach for georeferencing historical itineraries using a modern gazetteer. We combine textual information (historical toponyms) and spatial information (travel distances) into a hidden Markov model. Naively calculating a maximum likelihood explanation is slow, but careful algorithm engineering achieves high performance suitable for user interaction.

We demonstrate the practical potential of our approach by georeferencing 48 itineraries (containing 691 stops) from two important historical guidebooks published in 1563 and 1597: our approach is fast and accurate. Additionally, we show how sensitivity analysis can be used to power an efficient user interface for quality assurance.

6.1 Introduction

Historical itineraries are fascinating documents that convey spatial information from the past. They describe routes by listing encountered settlements along the way, often including the travel distance between them. Georeferencing these itineraries – that is, identifying the corresponding modern place for each historical stop – is a "tedious, but highly insightful" task that is not always undertaken [Krü74]. The main reason for not doing it is the amount of manual effort involved (using various sources of information, such as lexica and modern maps). Existing tools that support the process, while certainly useful, are insufficient to tip the balance for mass georeferencing: they merely provide visualization aids and usability improvements. The *Recogito* system [SBIdSC15], for example, provides a smooth user experience, but does not offer meaningful support for georeferencing itineraries.

In this chapter, we present a system that automates georeferencing historical itineraries to a large extent. This places our work in the scope of Chiang's research vision [Chi15] of an intelligent pipeline for handling historical spatial data. In particular, our algorithm is able to assign historical stops in the itinerary to modern places with high accuracy. Our main contribution are improvements in several respects over previous work on the same topic by Blank and Henrich [BH16a]. Their algorithm is an ad-hoc heuristic without reasonable runtime guarantee. In contrast, our algorithm is based on proper mathematical

---

This chapter is based on joint work with Thomas C. van Dijk [BvD17].

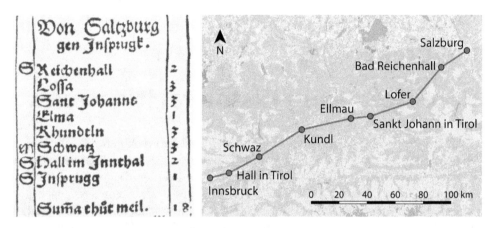

Figure 6.1: *Left:* itinerary from the *Raißbüchlin*, describing the route from Salzburg to Innsbruck. *Right:* the same route on a modern map, showing corresponding modern places.

modeling as an optimization problem. We give a polynomial-time algorithm to compute the optimal assignment and show that it is fast in practice. Additionally, we present an efficient user interaction for quality assurance, driven by sensitivity analysis.

Being able to automatically retrieve information from historical itineraries is beneficial for research practice, since a great number of historical itineraries remains in existence today. Some of the itineraries considered in the experiments in this chapter are taken from Jörg Gail's *Raißbüchlin*[1] [Krü74], a book of itineraries published in 1563. It contains 161 routes throughout Europe, with a focus on Southern Germany. The itineraries are given as a sequence of stops, each of which lists a place name and the travel distance from the previous stop. Some stops are also annotated with a class label that identifies them as a city, market town, village or monastery.

See Figure 6.1 (left) for Gail's itinerary from Salzburg to Innsbruck. Note that the destination Innsbruck is spelled in different ways even on this single page and neither time matches the modern spelling; in fact, none of the given toponyms equal their modern equivalents (right). Still, some phonetic similarity between corresponding place names is present, and the distances given on the right side of the page are plausible (at least in relation to each other).

The remainder of this chapter is organized as follows. First we discuss related work (Section 6.2). Then, we model the georeferencing task as an optimization problem (Section 6.3), for which we give an efficient algorithmic solution (Section 6.4). We experimentally evaluate our approach (Section 6.5) and apply it to the Raißbüchlin in a case study (Section 6.6). For quality assurance of the georeferenced result, we use sensitivity analysis and introduce an efficient user interaction (Section 6.7).

---

[1] Appropriately, *Raißbüchlin* literally translates to "travel book."

6.2   Related Work

The research presented in this chapter is related to various fields. Most closely related is a series of papers by Blank and Henrich, which we will discuss first.

Historical Itineraries and Gazetteers.   Blank and Henrich [BH15] recently introduced the problem of *itinerary resolution*, which they describe as a four-step process:

(1) optical character recognition,

(2) itinerary parsing,

(3) toponym resolution, and

(4) route finding.

By route finding, the authors mean the problem of finding the actual paths underlying a particular itinerary. In this chapter, we address the tasks from steps (1) and (3).

In a second paper, Blank and Henrich [BH16a] present a heuristic for step (3), matching an itinerary to a given gazetteer based on string distance and geometry. Their algorithm prunes the search space using textual and geospatial filters. This approach is reported to work well in practice, but lacks a clear optimization goal and has runtimes of several minutes. Addressing an audience from the humanities, a further paper [BH16b] presents another evaluation of this approach. However, in that paper, their approach is not very accurate on the itinerary used for demonstration.

In 1974, Krüger [Krü74] published a facsimile of the *Raißbüchlin*. This is our source for this document and the corresponding imagery in this present book. Together with the facsimile, Krüger provides an in-depth investigation of the *Raißbüchlin* in the context of contemporary itineraries from the perspective of historical road network research.

Southall et al. [SMB11] postulate the need for historical gazetteers, by which they mean gazetteers that are enriched with historical places and name variations. They survey existing gazetteers and discuss requirements from a historian's standpoint, many of which would also be helpful for the task discussed in this chapter. Note that our approach not only benefits from extensive historical gazetteers, but might actively help improve them by adding additional name variations (by georeferencing itineraries that contain previously unknown toponyms). Improving gazetteers in this way is known as gazetteer enrichment and is highly relevant to the spatial humanities: for an overview, see Berman et al. [BMS16].

Geocoding and Modern Itineraries.   Geocoding, that is, determining locations based on textual descriptions, is an active field of research in geographic information retrieval. For an extensive survey on automated geocoding of textual documents, see Melo and Martins [MM17].

In terms of modern itineraries, Moncla et al. [MGNIM16] introduce a system for reconstructing itineraries from annotated text, for example on a corpus of hiking descriptions [MRANG14]. Adelfio and Samet [AS14] present an approach to identify and extract modern route description from spreadsheets and websites.

Extracting itinerary information from unstructured input is relevant in the context of historical itineraries as well, since not all historical guidebooks have the tabular format of the *Raißbüchlin*. (This corresponds to step (2) in Blank and Henrich's [BH15] itinerary resolution process.) Still, many historical guidebooks exhibit structure that may enable the automatic extraction of the toponyms (for example: Khan et al. [KVW13]). In this chapter we assume that any such processing is already done and require the itinerary to be given as a list of toponyms and distances.

Historical Spellings. Handling historical spelling variants of toponyms is one of the main challenges in identifying corresponding modern places for itinerary entries. Ernst-Gerlach and Fuhr [EGF07] present a system for text retrieval supporting non-standard historical spellings. Rather than applying a manually-created set of rules, we *learn* transformations from a training corpus. For this we use a lexicon of historical spelling variants of places in Franconia compiled by von Reitzenstein [FvR09]; there are other similar databases, for example *THELO*[2] by the Academy of Sciences and Literature Mainz.

Butler et al. [BDTG17] recently gave an overview of historical onomastic variations of place names in the context of geotagging. In particular, the authors discuss common issues with place names from sources from the 17th to the 19th century and how non-standardized spelling makes automated place recognition challenging.

String Distances and Toponyms. There is some research on matching modern toponyms (to each other) based on string distance. Recchia and Louwerse [RL13] compare various string similarity measures in this context. Kılınç [Kıl16] presents an approximate string matching approach for toponym matching and shows that it outperforms some of the traditional string distance measures.

There is less research about matching historical toponyms to modern ones. Blank and Henrich [BH16a] evaluate 13 string distance measures on historical toponyms from itineraries. They conclude that on their data set, which consists of 15 routes from the *Raißbüchlin*, Levenshtein distance [Lev66], Jaro distance [Win90] and a distance measure based on the Cologne Phonetics [Pos69] perform best.

To suit our probabilistic model, we use the probabilistic string edit distance introduced by Ristad and Yianilos [RY98]. Their system has the advantage that it integrates well with our probabilistic modeling and can be trained for specific applications. In particular, we will be able to use existing material from the humanities (here: lexica of historical spelling variants) as training data for this system (see Section 6.6.2).

---

[2] http://www.personalschriften.de/datenbanken/thelo.html

Connection to Map Matching. There are some conceptual similarities between our itinerary resolution problem and the more well-known problem of map matching. The latter involves noisy GPS points with time stamps, and a known underlying road network. We do not have exactly that, but we do have noisy location information (from the historical place names), somewhat unreliable information about where to go next (through the reported distance between the stops), and an underlying gazetteer. In their landmark paper on map matching, Newson and Krumm present "a novel, principled map matching algorithm" [NK09]. Our algorithm is similarly based on a probabilistic model and finding a most-likely path in a hidden Markov model (HMM), but the ingredients to the model are fairly different. (Somewhat interestingly, Newson and Krumm's model has a complicated transition distribution, whereas ours has a complicated observation distribution.)

6.3   Problem Statement and Modeling

We now formalize the input to our georeferencing algorithm (which corresponds to step (3) of Blank and Henrich's itinerary resolution problem): an itinerary and a gazetteer.

- The itinerary $\mathcal{I}$ is a sequence of stops. Let $k = |\mathcal{I}|$. Each stop in the itinerary consists of a historical toponym (as a string) and a distance from the previous stop (a number). (In our modeling, we ignore possible settlement-type information.)

- The gazetteer $\mathcal{G}$ is a set of places. Let $n = |\mathcal{G}|$. Each place consists of a modern toponym (as a string) and a latitude/longitude pair. A gazetteer can contain additional information, such as modern-day population; we do not use this information. In case alternative or historical place names are available, we model these as additional gazetteer entries with the same geolocation.

This input contains several kinds of noise. Firstly, toponyms have changed over the centuries. Sometimes, they are seemingly unrelated at a string level (now it's Istanbul, not Constantinople): in this case the historical toponym must be in the gazetteer, otherwise we have no chance to georeference with high confidence based on the string alone. Luckily, in many cases the historical toponym is phonetically similar to the modern one. Transcription errors introduce further noise, but string similarity measures can be applied to some success.

The distances given in the itinerary are imprecise for a variety of reasons. It is not generally known what (if any) road network underlies the reported travel distances. The conversion factor between reported distances in the itinerary and real-world geodistances is also not necessarily clear: see Section 6.6.4 for a discussion. Furthermore, in our itineraries, many distances are given as integers between 1 and 5, which is rather coarse-grained. Still, these numbers clearly contain information about where to find the places on a modern map.

We now combine the textual and spatial information into a Bayesian model for georeferencing sets of itineraries. When restricted to a single itinerary, this model reduces to a hidden Markov model. Future work could consider the potential benefit of combining information from multiple itineraries, but will likely face a harder inference problem.

Consider a single itinerary. We introduce three variables for each stop in the itinerary: the historical toponym $\mathbf{T}_i$ (domain: strings), the reported distance from the previous stop $\mathbf{D}_i$ (domain: reals), and the modern place $\mathbf{P}_i$ (domain: gazetteer $\mathcal{G}$). We have observed the first two variables at each stop and the third variable gives the solution to our problem. We will infer a most likely assignment. It may be noted that $\mathbf{T}_i$ and $\mathbf{D}_i$ have infinite domain, but this is not a problem since we have observed these variables and therefore they have singleton support.

As a modeling decision, we postulate the following independences. Conditioned on $\mathbf{P}_i$, that is, given a decision to georeference step i as a certain place:

- other places are conditionally independent of $\mathbf{T}_i$ and $\mathbf{D}_i$: if we have decided on a place, it no longer matters what the itinerary says for that stop;

- later places are conditionally independent of all places before $\mathbf{P}_i$, i.e., $\mathbf{P}$ is Markov: if we have decided a place, going forward it does not matter what came before; and,

- the previous place $\mathbf{P}_{i-1}$ combined with the distance $\mathbf{D}_i$ is conditionally independent of $\mathbf{T}_i$: our a priori assessment of how historical and modern toponyms relate is independent of our a priori assessment of how reported distances in the itinerary relate to geodistances.

We start from a uniform prior on each of the place variables $\mathbf{P}_i$ and then *fuse* our evidence [Pea86] using the conditional probability distributions given in the next three subsections. Each one can be fused separately because of the assumed independences.

6.3.1 Toponym Evidence

The influence of the historical toponym on the selected place is achieved through an evidential term $\mathbb{P}_t(\mathbf{P}_i | \mathbf{T}_i)$, that is, the a priori conditional probability distribution over places in the gazetteer given a historical toponym. We set this distribution based on the modern toponyms in the gazetteer and the statistical string similarity measure of Ristad and Yianilos [RY98]. Their similarity measure has the advantage of being rigorously grounded in probability theory and being trainable by expectation maximization on an appropriate corpus. With $t_{\text{modern}}(\mathbf{P}_i)$ the modern toponym of place $\mathbf{P}_i$, and $\text{sim}_{\text{RY}}(\cdot, \cdot)$ the Ristad-Yianilos similarity, we let

$$\mathbb{P}_t(\mathbf{P}_i | \mathbf{T}_i) \overset{\Delta}{=} \text{sim}_{\text{RY}}(t_{\text{modern}}(\mathbf{P}_i), \mathbf{T}_i). \tag{6.1}$$

Note that $\mathbf{T}_i$ is in fact observed: we set it equal to the historical toponym at stop i.

The basic version of Ristad and Yianilos's measure favors short strings over long ones. Since we need to assess the similarity of strings of various lengths, this version of the measure is not suitable for our application. Instead, we use their alternate model conditioned on length [RY98, Appendix B] that does not have this issue, but depends on a joint probability distribution over the lengths of two strings. Ristad and Yianilos do not give such a distribution; we define our own distribution that fits the data from our application well (look ahead at Figure 6.5).

We use the following joint probability distribution over the length ℓ_m of a modern toponym t_m and the length ℓ_h of a historical toponym t_h. Each character in t_m is independently counted as either zero, one, or two, with probabilities p_0, p_1, and $p_2 = 1 - p_0 - p_1$. We define the probability that this sum equals the ℓ_h to be the joint probability of the lengths of t_m and t_h.

In the process described above, let k_0, k_1, and k_2 denote the number of times a character is counted as zero, one, or two, respectively. Observe that $\ell_m = k_0 + k_1 + k_2$, $\ell_h = k_1 + 2k_2$, and $k_2 = \ell_h - \ell_m + k_0$. The joint probability over the lengths of the two toponyms can then be calculated as

$$\mathbb{P}(\ell_m, \ell_h) = \sum_{k_0=0}^{\ell_m} \sum_{k_1=0}^{\ell_m-k_0} \binom{\ell_m}{k_0} \binom{\ell_m - k_0}{k_1} p_0^{k_0} p_1^{k_1} p_2^{k_2}. \tag{6.2}$$

Training the similarity measure and choosing appropriate values for p_0 and p_1 is discussed in Section 6.6.2.

6.3.2 Distance Evidence

The influence of distance information on the selected place is achieved through an evidential term $\mathbb{P}_d(\mathbf{P}_i | \mathbf{P}_{i-1}, \mathbf{D}_i)$. Here we consider two consecutive places and the reported distance between them. Through the gazetteer's latitude/longitude pairs, we can calculate the distance between these two places. (In the absence of information about a historical road network, we take the great-circle distance.)

We assume that the reported historical and the calculated modern distance are approximately equal: we set the relative probabilities of places based on a normal distribution around an expected difference of zero. Here it is relevant that $\mathbf{D}_i$ is given in historical units: we multiply by some constant conversion factor λ to get modern units. (We will see in Section 6.6.4 that $\lambda = 7.5$ works well for the historical German miles in the test itineraries.)

With dist$(\cdot, \cdot)$ the great-circle distance (in kilometers), and $\mathcal{N}(\cdot; \sigma)$ the normal distribution around zero with standard deviation σ, we let

$$\mathbb{P}_d(\mathbf{P}_i | \mathbf{P}_{i-1}, \mathbf{D}_i) \stackrel{\Delta}{=} \mathcal{N}(\text{dist}(\mathbf{P}_{i-1}, \mathbf{P}) - \lambda \cdot \mathbf{D}_i ; \sigma_d). \tag{6.3}$$

The value of σ_d is discussed in Section 6.4.1. Note that $\mathbf{D}_i$ and $\mathbf{P}_{i-1}$ are known constants when evaluating this expression.

It is, in principle, possible to include the conversion factor λ as a variable in the model to be inferred. However, this makes exact inference infeasible since all $\mathbf{P}_i$ become dependent. A MLESAC-based approach like that of Weinman [Wei13] could work, but we have not found picking λ to be a problem in practice.

6.3.3 Bearing Evidence

An additional spatial term can be based on the bearing from $\mathbf{P}_{i-1}$ to $\mathbf{P}_i$. We take this to be independent of the other evidence terms. This term is optional, though we find that our most-accurate results are achieved with this term included.

Many historical itineraries describe routes with a fairly consistent bearing [BH16b]. If we are given some overall bearing B for the route, then any two consecutive places should have approximately this bearing. We model this using an evidential term $\mathbb{P}_b(\mathbf{P}_i \mid \mathbf{P}_{i-1})$. With bear$(\cdot, \cdot)$ the initial geodetic bearing from the first to the second place (in degrees), diff$(\cdot, \cdot)$ the difference between two bearings, and $\mathcal{N}(\cdot; \sigma)$ as before, we let

$$\mathbb{P}_b(\mathbf{P}_i \mid \mathbf{P}_{i-1}) \triangleq \mathcal{N}(\text{diff}(\text{bear}(\mathbf{P}_{i-1}, \mathbf{P}), B); \sigma_b). \tag{6.4}$$

The value of σ_b is discussed in Section 6.4.1.

The input as specified before does not contain B, but we can get reasonable values in various ways. We may require the user to pick a bearing, for example using a rough dragging gesture in a graphical user interface. Alternatively, we could hope to georeference the first and the last stop based purely on string similarity, since they are often major cities. In our experiments in Section 6.5, we have used the initial bearing from first to last place, which we have manually georeferenced for this purpose. (We present experiments with and without bearing information.)

6.3.4 Representation as Hidden Markov Model

The Bayesian model above has an intuitive interpretation as a hidden Markov model: there is a historical journey (a sequence of actual places) that we have not observed, and these places have "emitted" observations in the form of historical toponyms written down in the itinerary. The reported distances and the bearing information are both expressed by the transition probabilities between hidden states. Putting some evidence in the emissions and some in the transitions is justified since the resulting inference procedure for $\mathbf{P}_i$ is equivalent to the fusion rules of Bayesian inference [Pea86].

As hidden states, we take the places $\mathbf{P}_i$. Each has as domain all places in gazetteer $\mathcal{G}$. It remains to specify the transition distributions $\mathbb{P}(\mathbf{P}_i \mid \mathbf{P}_{i-1})$ and the emission distributions $\mathbb{P}(\mathbf{T}_i \mid \mathbf{P}_i)$. The emission distribution is given through the toponym evidence term:

$$\mathbb{P}(\mathbf{T}_i \mid \mathbf{P}_i) \triangleq \text{sim}_{RY}(\mathbf{T}_i, t_{\text{modern}}(\mathbf{P}_i)). \tag{6.5}$$

Note that the arguments to the string similarity function are flipped compared to Equation (6.1).

The transition distributions are given by multiplying the distance and bearing evidence, which is valid by their assumed independence. Let $e_d = \text{dist}(\mathbf{P}_{i-1}, \mathbf{P}) - \lambda \cdot \mathbf{D}_i$ and $e_b = \text{diff}(\text{bear}(\mathbf{P}_{i-1}, \mathbf{P}), B)$. Then:

$$\mathbb{P}(\mathbf{P}_i \mid \mathbf{P}_{i-1}) \triangleq \mathcal{N}(e_d; \sigma_d) \cdot \mathcal{N}(e_b; \sigma_b). \tag{6.6}$$

We take the prior distribution over the states to be uniform. This completes our model: for this hidden Markov model we compute a maximum-likelihood sequence of states and this is our georeferenced output: a globally most-likely set of values $\mathbf{P}_i$ incorporating all evidence.

To recap, the model requires as input all historical toponyms $\mathbf{T}_i$ and reported distances $\mathbf{D}_i$. It requires a distance conversion factor λ and, if available, takes an overall bearing B.

6.4 Algorithm Engineering

Inference in HMMs can famously be done using the Viterbi algorithm [Vit67]. Directly applying it to our HMM yields the following.

Theorem 6.1. *A most-likely sequence of places can be computed in $O(kn^2)$ time and $O(kn)$ space.*

Our HMM has the curious property that the Markov chain is short (k stops), but the state space is large (n gazetteer entries). This is reversed from the common situation and is unfortunate for the runtime, since the dependence on n is quadratic.

All algorithms were implemented in C++ and the experiments were run on an Intel® Core™ i5-4670 CPU at 3.4 GHz with 8 GB of RAM running Ubuntu 14.04. We first report on a straightforward implementation of the Viterbi algorithm and then report several improvements based on some of the peculiarities of our model and data. The algorithmic and engineering improvements in this section achieve a speedup in excess of two orders of magnitude.

6.4.1 Textbook Viterbi

As baseline we have implemented the "textbook" version of the Viterbi algorithm: eagerly filling a table of dynamic-programming values and back pointers. There are $O(kn)$ states and each takes $O(n)$ time to evaluate since the algorithm considers all previous states.

We are solely interested in the most-likely path and not its actual probability. Hence we need not normalize the transition distributions: every sequence of states involves exactly one term from each distribution $\mathbb{P}(\mathbf{P}_i \mid \mathbf{P}_{i-1})$, so all paths are off by the same factor (namely the product of all missing normalization constants).

Next we apply the well-known transformation of taking logarithms and using addition, rather than working with raw probabilities and multiplication. Recall that the transition distribution $\mathbb{P}(\mathbf{P}_i \mid \mathbf{P}_{i-1})$ is the product of two normal distributions (distance and bearing). Taking Equation (6.6) and expanding the normal distributions, we get:

$$\mathbb{P}(\mathbf{P}_i \mid \mathbf{P}_{i-1}) \overset{\Delta}{=} \frac{1}{\sqrt{2\pi\sigma_d^2}} \cdot \exp\left(\frac{-e_d^2}{2\sigma_d^2}\right) \cdot \frac{1}{\sqrt{2\pi\sigma_b^2}} \cdot \exp\left(\frac{-e_b^2}{2\sigma_b^2}\right). \tag{6.7}$$

Similarly to the normalization factors, we can drop the first and third factor since they are constant everywhere. Then, taking logarithms cancels the exponentiation and turns multiplication into addition. This leaves $-e_d^2/2\sigma_d^2 - e_b^2/2\sigma_b^2$. Here we see that σ_d and σ_b act as inverse weights on the corresponding error term. In the remainder of the chapter, let $\delta = 1/2\sigma_d^2$ and $\beta = 1/2\sigma_b^2$: it is more convenient to discuss linear weight factors. When we later experimentally pick good values for δ and β, the above relation gives us the implied standard deviations.

After these transformations, the values computed by the Viterbi algorithm are not easily and directly interpretable as probabilities. However, as argued above, these values suffice for our purpose, namely determining the most-likely path. From now on we refer to these values as *Viterbi values*.

The Viterbi algorithm considers for every pair of places the distance and bearing between them: we can precompute a complete lookup table. This does not improve the asymptotic runtime (clearly these computations take constant time each), but building the lookup table can be trivially parallelized. Using a single OpenMP [DM98] directive, we achieve near-100% utilization of our quadcore machine while filling the table, giving a 3.96-fold speedup of this step. As a downside, this table increases the memory usage from $O(kn)$ to $\Omega(n^2)$. This can be an obstacle in practice: for example at $n = 24\,000$ the tables exceed 4 GB each when stored at double precision.

On one of our larger (but otherwise typical) instances ($k = 18$, $n \approx 10\,000$), our basic implementation takes 698.8 s. A more careful implementation of the evaluation of dynamic-programming states leads to 68.5 s runtime.[3] Eliding exponentiation results in a runtime of 30.0 s. We use this version as our baseline implementation in Section 6.5.

Adding the lookup table with multithreaded precomputation gives runtime 12.9 s. The next algorithm will improve this further to 2.6 s, but for ease of implementation one might prefer the algorithm described in this section.

6.4.2 Lazy Evaluation

Calculating a most-likely path in a hidden Markov model can be modeled as finding a longest path in a directed acyclic graph called a *trellis* (see for example [BCJR74]). This observation suggests a Dijkstra-like search based on a priority queue. In the coding-theory community, such algorithms are called "lazy Viterbi" [HHC93, FAFF02], since they do not necessarily evaluate all states. In this setting, we do not precompute lookup tables for distances and bearings, since we hope that we do not have to know most of these values for computing a longest path.

---

[3] When evaluating a dynamic programming state we have to loop over the possible preceding states and keep a running maximum of where the best value comes from. If the dynamic-programming value of that state is already lower than our running maximum, we can conclude that this state will not improve our value, since all transition costs are negative. Then we do not need to calculate the distance and bearing terms for this transition. We similarly elide calculation of the bearing term if the distance term shows that this preceding state is useless.

When using the lazy approach, the worst-case runtime in general suffers by a factor $O(\log n)$ because of priority-queue operations, but since fewer nodes are inspected in practice, the actual runtime improves. For a significant improvement, the edge weights should be transformed as described by Feldman et al. [FAFF02]: between any two layers in the trellis, add a constant to each weight such that the maximum over the edge weights between these layers becomes 0. (As argued before, this is safe since we add the same constants to all paths, which does not influence which path is optimal.) We additionally implemented bidirectional search on this trellis.

On the same large instance as before, the basic lazy algorithm runs in 13.3 s: slightly slower than our best implementation of "eager" Viterbi. After adjusting the edge weights as described, this improves to 4.6 s. Bidirectional search improves this further to 2.6 s. Unfortunately, bidirectional search is not consistently faster on all of our itineraries. Still, it is on average a small improvement (look ahead at Table 6.4). Future work could investigate improved search strategies.

6.4.3 A Heuristic

As a heuristic to further improve runtimes, we can filter the gazetteer based on string similarity, rejecting most states as implausible. We do this by restricting the domain of each $\mathbf{P}_i$ to the τ most string-similar entries at that stop. The algorithm first finds appropriate gazetteer entries by brute force, and then runs the eager Viterbi algorithm. This gives the following.

Theorem 6.2. *The most-likely sequence of places, restricted to the top-τ places at each stop, can be computed in $O(k\tau^2 + kn)$ time and $O(k\tau)$ memory.*

This is a significant improvement over the runtimes of the exact algorithms discussed before, since the reduction is in the quadratic term. The disadvantage is that we are no longer guaranteed to find an optimal solution (to the original problem; clearly we find an optimal solution to this restricted problem). In Section 6.5.3 we evaluate suitable values of τ for cases where speed is more important than quality. This can for example be the case in a system with real-time user interaction: we can quickly present a first result based on a low-τ solution, and then run the full inference in the background.

Taking the top τ states is a rank-based filter; it is also possible to filter with a similarity threshold. Potentially this could be a more sensible threshold, but does not give a predictably-low runtime like the rank filter.

6.4.4 Sensitivity Analysis

Consider a stop i and let its most-likely assignment be $\mathbf{P}_i = g^*$, for some place $g^* \in \mathcal{G}$. We can find a "second-best" solution by computing the most-likely assignment for $\mathbf{P}_i$ conditioned on $\mathbf{P}_i \neq g^*$. (In general, this may also affect the most-likely assignment of other stops.) If this alternative solution has almost the same Viterbi value, the output of the algorithm could have easily been different if the input had been slightly different: this does not inspire confidence in the solution. On the other hand, if the alternative solution is much worse, the solution is robust in the sense that there is no closely competing alternate solution. These sensitivity values can be used to power an interactive user interface for quality assurance: see Section 6.7. Here we discuss the efficient computation of these values.

We can calculate the above second-best sensitivity by running any of the previous algorithms and making it skip the possibility that $\mathbf{P}_i = g^*$. Doing this for each stop in the itinerary takes $O(k^2 n^2)$ time. We can do better with a variant of the eager Viterbi algorithm – this will have worse constant factors than the algorithms discussed before, but the asymptotic improvement makes up for this.

Theorem 6.3. *The Viterbi values of the most-likely sequence of places, conditioned on* $\mathbf{P}_i = g$, *can be calculated for all* $1 \leq i \leq k$ *and all* $g \in G$ *in a total of* $O(kn^2)$ *time and* $O(kn)$ *space.*

Proof (sketch). Run the eager Viterbi algorithm twice, once as normal and once with the itinerary reversed, and keep both dynamic-programming tables. This is within the time and space bounds. Then for any i and g, the conditional Viterbi value for $\mathbf{P}_i = g$ can be read from the dynamic-programming tables by adding the forward value of "stop i equals g" to the value in the other direction (taking care not to count stop i twice). This takes $O(1)$ time per combination of a stop and a place, which again falls within the time bound. ☐

This result also gives us the second-best solution for each stop simply by inspecting all places for a fixed stop and taking the second best.

6.5 Experiments

We evaluate our model on real-world data from two historical guidebooks: Gail's *Raißbüchlin* from 1563 as taken from Krüger's facsimile [Krü74] and the anonymously published *Kronn und Auszbunde aller Wegweiser* [Ano97] from 1597. For the sake of brevity, we refer to the latter as the *Kronn* for the remainder of this chapter. We work with three sets of itineraries taken from these publications:

RB1: 21 routes from first 35 pages of the *Raißbüchlin*,

RB2: a selection of 15 edited routes from the *Raißbüchlin* used by Blank and Henrich [BH16a], and

KR: the 12 routes originating in Würzburg from the *Kronn*.

For RB1 and KR, we manually created ground truth, identifying a gazetteer entry for each stop; we did not edit or cut the routes. For comparison we include the data set RB2, which was used by Blank and Henrich. (Some of their itineraries do not match the source

Table 6.1: Overview of the three data sets. Lengths are calculated according to the ground-truth modern places.

data set	RB1	RB2	KR
source	*Raißbüchlin*	*Raißbüchlin*	*Kronn*
year of publication	1563	1563	1597
# of itineraries	21	15	12
total # of stops	354	218	119
median # of stops	14	14	10
unidentified stops	5	3	8
total length [km]	5552 km	3052 km	1480 km
median length	210 km	179 km	104 km

Table 6.2: Statistics of the two gazetteer sources used for experimentation. For each of the three (itinerary) data sets, the average number of entries in the bounding box of an itinerary is given. In addition, the table shows the total number of entries for all itineraries of the three data sets.

gazetteer source	∅ RB1	∅ RB2	∅ KR	total
GeoNames	6342.1	3798.5	1881.3	212 737
Getty TGN	4736.4	3781.4	2028.3	180 524

material exactly: some are reversed and some cover only part of a *Raißbüchlin* itinerary.) In all three data sets, there is a small number of stops for which we could not identify a gazetteer entry, most likely due to deserted villages. For these, we accepted any solution. See Table 6.1 for an overview of the data sets. These data sets are culturally and temporally specific, but do note that our system can (and should) be trained on appropriate data: to georeference for example Latin itineraries, one should train the string similarity on different data and use a different distance conversion factor λ.

We have used two different publicly available sources to generate our input gazetteers: the GeoNames geographic database[4] and the Getty Thesaurus of Geographic Names[5] (Getty TGN). For each itinerary individually, we constructed a gazetteer by extracting the set of places from either source in a bounding box around the itinerary, padded by 0.1° latitude and longitude. This selection step requires a rough knowledge of where the described route is located. This is a reasonable assumption, since the place of departure and the destination are given in the title of each itinerary, and are usually well-known cities. Blank and Henrich [BH16a] describe a very similar selection step based on the same assumption. See Table 6.2 for an overview.

---

[4] http://www.geonames.org/
[5] http://www.getty.edu/research/tools/vocabularies/tgn/index.html

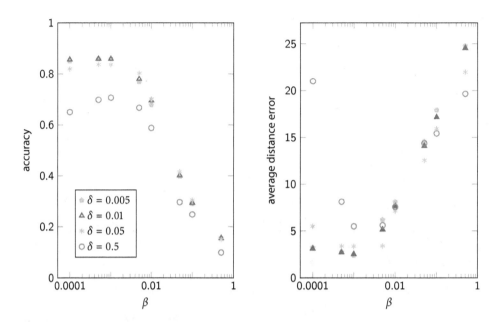

Figure 6.2: Different parameter values on RB1 using GeoNames. Both the highest accuracy (85.9%) and lowest distance error (2.4 km) are achieved with $\delta = 0.005$ and $\beta = 0.001$.

For the experiments presented in this section, we assume all input data has been correctly parsed, organized as an itinerary $\mathcal{I}$, and that our string distance measure has been appropriately trained. Section 6.6 describes how this was achieved.

6.5.1 Parameter Choice

We begin by discussing the choice of the parameters, in particular δ and β, and their impact on the quality of the solution. We measure the accuracy (that is, the fraction of places that are assigned correctly) and a distance error: the average distance between the assigned place and the correct place according to ground truth (which is zero for correctly-assigned places).

For **RB1** in combination with GeoNames gazetteers, we can pick parameters ($\delta = 0.005$, $\beta = 0.001$) that achieve 85.9% accuracy and a low average distance error (2.4 km). In fact, the algorithm is quite robust in terms of parameter choice: there is an interval of about an order of magnitude for both δ and β in which any combination of the two parameters yields accuracy values greater than 80% (see Figure 6.2). For these intervals of parameter values, the average distance error stays below 3.5 km.

Figure 6.3 (left) shows a solution computed by our algorithm. It contains a single error: a place given as "Jesta" in the itinerary in fact corresponds to the modern place Oestheim, while the algorithm picks Esbach. Note the significant change in the place name; still, the distances and bearing allowed the algorithm to pick a place that is geo-

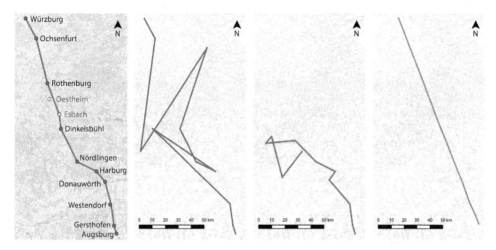

Figure 6.3: Route from Augsburg to Würzburg. The map on the far left shows the solution with recommended parameters (red) and one error (the yellow places). The remaining three maps show a solution using no spatial evidence (blue), too much weight on distance ($\delta = 1$, red), and too much weight on bearing ($\beta = 1$, green). Points in the background indicate gazetteer places.

graphically plausible. Elsewhere on the route, the algorithm was able to correctly assign Donauwörth ("Thonawerdt") and Dinkelsbühl ("Dinckelspihel").

Using GeoNames gazetteers, the algorithm achieves high accuracy on the remaining data sets as well; see Table 6.3 for details. This shows that our approach is able to generate accurate solutions for various combinations of itineraries and gazetteers, and that it is somewhat robust in terms of parameter choice: based on our experiments, we recommend setting $\delta = 0.05$ and $\beta = 0.001$ for previously unseen data sets. This is a clear methodological improvement over Blank and Henrich, who achieve similar accuracy, but only if researchers "adequately choose the parameters" for each itinerary individually [BH16a].

In fact, Blank and Henrich's paper [BH16a] leads us to believe there does not exist a consistently-good set of parameters for their algorithm. In their experiments, they report an accuracy of 83.7% on data set RB2, but use individually tuned sets of parameters for each of the 15 itineraries: the authors do not report results for a consistent set of parameters. In addition, they run their algorithm in three different modes for each itinerary and only count the best result. Note in particular that their parameters and modes can only be evaluated using the ground truth, which is of course not available in practical applications. Reporting on a consistent choice of mode, the best choice leads to an accuracy of 71.2% (still allowing individual parameters for each itinerary). Our approach clearly outperforms this result with a global set of parameters.

Next, we briefly consider extreme choices for the parameters. Disabling the distance and bearing terms leads the algorithm to greedily assign each stop independently to the most string-similar place. This results in much lower accuracy (64.97% for RB1 using

Table 6.3: *Top:* parameters that achieve the best accuracy on each data set, with the corresponding distance error. *Bottom:* the same measures, but with our recommended parameter set.

data set	GeoNames			Getty		
	RB1	RB2	KR	RB1	RB2	KR
distance factor δ	0.005	0.05	0.05	0.005	0.05	0.05
bearing factor β	0.001	0.005	0.001	0.001	0.005	0.001
accuracy	85.9%	82.1%	86.6%	70.6%	73.4%	77.3%
distance error [km]	2.4	1.3	2.6	4.1	2.0	2.2
With recommended values $\delta = 0.05$ and $\beta = 0.001$:						
accuracy	83.6%	80.7%	86.6%	68.6%	70.2%	77.3%
distance error [km]	3.3	1.3	2.6	4.1	2.2	2.2

GeoNames), demonstrating that the spatial evidence is useful and successfully integrated. In the other extreme, putting too much weight on a particular factor is also detrimental. For RB1 and GeoNames, Figure 6.2 shows the results of $\delta = 1$ and $\beta = 1$, which pushes the accuracy considerably below 40%. We see in Figure 6.3 (right) that extreme parameter values indeed lead to nonsensical solutions.

Recall that in the present experiments, we assume the initial bearing from first to last place to be known, but the global bearing of the itineraries might in practice as well be unknown. When we do not take bearing information into account, the accuracy for RB1 using GeoNames itineraries slightly decreases, from 85.9% to 82.2%. This shows that bearing information does help increase accuracy, but is not absolutely required to achieve good results. Our approach is thus not limited to itineraries following a relatively straight route, but could handle for example round trips as well.

6.5.2 GeoNames vs. Getty TGN

For all three sets of itineraries, our algorithm is less accurate when run with the Getty-based gazetteers rather than those based on GeoNames: see Table 6.3. Except on KR, the distance errors are also higher. There are several factors leading to this behavior. First, the geo-coordinates given by Getty are quite imprecise; indeed, the Getty trust states that the gazetteer service it provides "is not a GIS" and the coordinates are meant for personal reference only.[6] Second, the gazetteers based on Getty are particularly sparse outside of Germany. This affects RB1, which includes several itineraries to Vienna and Prague. Despite these shortcomings of the Getty gazetteers, our algorithm still achieves accuracy upwards of 70%.

---

[6] http://www.getty.edu/research/tools/vocabularies/obtain/download.html

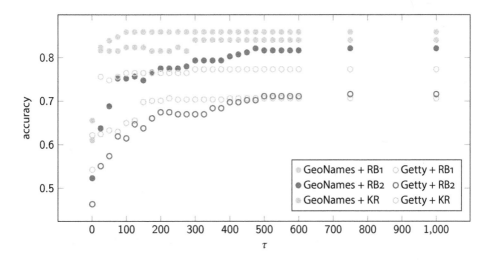

Figure 6.4: Accuracy of the heuristic as a function of the threshold τ.

6.5.3 Quality of the Heuristic Algorithm

In Section 6.4.3 we presented a fast, heuristic algorithm. For evaluating this algorithm, we use the parameters δ and β that performed best in our discussion in Section 6.5.1. Considering Figure 6.4, we see that all sets of itineraries and both gazetteers can be run with $\tau \approx 500$ quite successfully: the heuristic achieves accuracy within 0.5 percentage points of the exact algorithm. A more restrictive choice of $\tau = 200$ still yields accuracy within 5 percentage points. The improvement in runtime is discussed in the next section.

6.5.4 Runtime

We have run each algorithm on all six combinations of a set of itineraries and a gazetteer source, using the parameter set that yields the best accuracy for this pair. Table 6.4 gives the average runtime measured in these experiments.

As a baseline we have run all data sets with the "textbook" version of the Viterbi algorithm. The baseline is outperformed by all variants of our algorithm, except for "sensitivity", which calculates additional information. The lazy variant is on our data on average faster than the baseline by approximately a factor 4 and is, in turn, slightly outperformed by the bidirectional lazy algorithm. The two versions of the heuristic are faster than the exact approaches by a full order of magnitude. Runtime in the low tenths-of-a-second range mean the heuristic can be used in real-time interactive applications.

Processing itineraries from RB1 takes the longest on average. This is because RB1 contains several itineraries that span a large geographic area and consequently require a large gazetteer. For example, the bidirectional lazy algorithm takes 33 seconds to process an itinerary from Innsbruck to Vienna containing 24 stops using a GeoNames gazetteer

Table 6.4: Average runtime in seconds for one itinerary with the different variants of our algorithm.

	GeoNames			Getty		
data set	RB1	RB2	KR	RB1	RB2	KR
textbook Viterbi	24.88	8.83	2.77	13.46	8.72	2.80
lazy	6.44	2.19	0.45	3.92	2.26	0.58
bidirectional lazy	6.08	2.05	0.38	3.83	2.25	0.49
heuristic ($\tau = 500$)	0.21	0.15	0.06	0.18	0.15	0.06
heuristic ($\tau = 200$)	0.17	0.09	0.04	0.13	0.09	0.04
"sensitivity"	28.55	7.26	2.39	14.89	7.23	2.38

of size $n = 16\,129$. On the other hand, the same algorithm solves a further 11 itineraries from this data set in less than 0.2 seconds each.

All variants of our algorithm clearly outperform the algorithm by Blank and Henrich [BH16a], who report runtimes of 120 seconds for single itineraries from RB2.

6.6 Case Study: Data Preparation

In this section, we discuss important data preparation steps necessary to run our algorithm on real-world data. These steps are:

- optical character recognition for extracting the input for our algorithm from scans,
- training string similarity weights for use in $\mathbb{P}(\mathbf{T}_i \,|\, \mathbf{P}_i)$, and
- obtaining suitable gazetteer data.

In addition, we discuss picking a conversion factor from historical units of length to kilometers. We describe our approach to the data preparation as a case study on the *Raißbüchlin*, for which we thereby obtain a nearly complete digitization pipeline.

6.6.1 Manual Transcription vs. OCR

For the experiments described in Section 6.5, we have manually transcribed the input itineraries. In order to efficiently deal with large sets of itineraries, one might consider applying optical character recognition (OCR), which we discuss below. Alternatively, one could crowdsource the task and have volunteers transcribe the itineraries. There are indeed some successful crowdsourcing projects that focus specifically on transcribing historical documents.[7] We have not further investigated the applicability of crowdsourcing in the context of historical guidebooks; this would be an interesting direction for future work.

---

[7] `http://scribeproject.github.io/`

Höhn has applied his work-in-progress OCR system [Höh17] to our scans of the *Raißbüchlin*, in particular to the pages covering the itineraries in RB1. From the resulting text representation, we (manually) selected the 354 lines that correspond to itinerary stops. Note that this manual task corresponds to step (2) in Blank and Henrich's [BH15] definition of the itinerary resolution process.

The OCR system was trained on 9 of the 21 itineraries and achieves a character error rate of approximately 5% on previously unseen text from the *Raißbüchlin*. Evaluating the remaining 12 itineraries (151 stops), our algorithm achieves 76.8% accuracy, compared to 86.0% on a manual transcription of these 12 itineraries.[8] This is far from a comprehensive study of the performance OCR approaches could have in this domain. Instead, it is a promising proof of concept that shows the general applicability of OCR to the problem.

6.6.2 Training the String Similarity Measure

The statistical string similarity measure of Ristad and Yianilos [RY98] mentioned in Section 6.3.1 relies on a transition model learned from training data. The similarity measure can thus be tailored to a specific domain when provided with a sufficient number of appropriate training examples. In our case, this domain is matching corresponding historical and modern German toponyms. We used von Reitzenstein's lexicon of Franconian place names [FvR09] for this purpose. The lexicon contains approximately 800 entries of modern places and lists historical name variations for each of them. In total, we obtained 6432 pairs of corresponding modern and historical spellings from this lexicon.

Based on the same data, we pick parameters for our probability distribution over string lengths. Figure 6.5 shows some length distributions of historical toponyms (corresponding to modern toponyms of a given length). We chose p_0, p_1 and p_2 from Equation 6.2 to approximate these distributions. We manually tuned these parameter values and arrived at $p_0 = 0.07$, $p_1 = 0.85$, and consequently $p_2 = 0.08$. The resulting distribution is also presented in Figure 6.5; our model slightly overestimates small changes in length (fewer than two characters).

Interestingly, for modern toponyms of more than 12 characters, our data contains a considerable number of historical toponyms of much smaller length. (See the plot for modern toponyms of length 13 in Figure 6.5.) This is mostly caused by modern toponyms that are compound names and have corresponding historical toponyms that only consist of one part of the compound. Since less than 15% of the modern toponyms in our data have more than 12 characters, this is not a crucial problem in practice. Also, in such cases a (shorter) historical toponym might be present as an alternative place name in the gazetteer.

---

[8] Using slightly different parameters than those used with the manual transcription, our algorithm is able to achieve 78.2% accuracy with the OCR results.

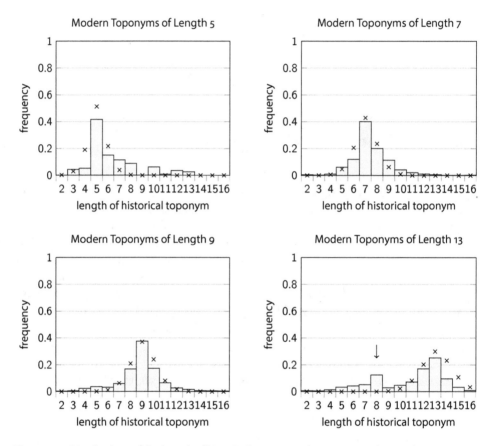

Figure 6.5: Distributions of the length of historical toponyms that correspond to modern toponyms of a given length. The crosses indicate our model with parameters $p_0 = 0.07$, $p_1 = 0.85$, and $p_2 = 0.08$. Note that for modern toponyms of length 13, a considerable number of corresponding historical toponym has length 8 (which is underestimated by our model). This is often due to modern compound toponyms corresponding to historical toponyms that only consist of one part of the compound.

6.6.3 Gazetteer and Itinerary Preparation

As mentioned before, we have based our gazetteers on two sources: GeoNames and Getty TGN. Both gazetteer sources are openly available: GeoNames offers SQL dumps[9] and Getty provides a SPARQL endpoint.[10]

As a first step, we have filtered the databases for entries that correspond to populated places. Both databases contain alternative names for places; in the case of Getty, we have included all of them. With GeoNames, alternative names are often tagged with a language, so we selected only German ones. There is a trade-off between having many toponym variants in the gazetteer (which means more, but possibly confusing information) and having a small gazetteer (better runtime, but possibly missing relevant information).

We apply a set of simple transformations to all toponyms, both from the gazetteers and the itineraries, in order to somewhat normalize them. Our transformations include dropping strings that are excessively long or contain characters that are implausible for our domain (for example non-western characters). Then we tokenize each place name (splitting on whitespace) and keep only the first token, with two exceptions. If the token is part of a stop list containing prepositions like "gen" ("toward"), we drop it and continue to the next token. If the token is part of a second list containing common prefixes like "Markt" or "St.", we merge it with the token after it. For example "gen markt bibart" becomes "marktbibart." Finally, we remove diacritics and replace special characters with similar standard characters.

Unfortunately, these transformations are rather ad-hoc and future work could attempt to put this step on proper foundation. At present it is necessary for two reasons. First, both gazetteer sources contain quite a number of malformed or incorrectly tagged place names. (For an in-depth evaluation of the inaccuracies to be encountered in GeoNames, see Ahlers [Ahl13].) With the tokenization, we try to fix these problematic entries. Second, the character set in the gazetteers must match the character set in the training data for our string distance measure. This is guaranteed by the replacement step.

In practice, it would be beneficial if a person with (historical) domain knowledge defined these transformation rules. Note that this person does not need to have a background in computer science; the rules for our data are mostly simple search-and-replace.

6.6.4 Conversion Factor for German Miles

In both the *Raißbüchlin* and *Kronn*, distances between stops are given in historical German miles. According to the literature [vA57], one historical German mile corresponds to 10 000 steps, which meant a travel time of approximately 2 hours by foot, and a conversion factor to kilometers of roughly $\lambda = 7.5$.

---

[9] http://download.geonames.org/export/dump/
[10] http://vocab.getty.edu/sparql

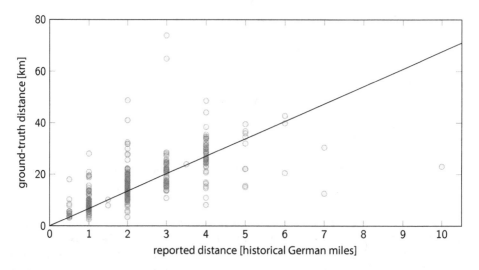

Figure 6.6: Reported distances from RB1 in comparison to the geodistances between the corresponding places from the ground truth (blue circles). The black line indicates the least-squares fit (with a fixed intercept of 0) for the data (λ = 6.767).

We have verified this conversion factor using a least-squares fit between the reported distances and the ground truth (assuming great-circle distances). This results in λ values of 6.767 for RB1, 7.259 for RB2, and 7.373 for KR. (Figure 6.6 shows the data for RB1.) Our algorithm is robust against such inaccuracies: for example, the georeferencing results on RB1 are the same for λ = 6.767 and λ = 7.5. We have used λ = 7.5 for all other experiments.

Note that it is not surprising that the empirical values of λ based on our data sets are lower than the value from the literature: the literature assumes great-circle distance, which will always underestimate the actual (historical) travel distance.

6.7 Smart User Interaction

In Section 6.5, we have shown that our algorithm typically works accurately, but does not always get all places right. Indeed, for the given problem an accuracy of 100% can hardly be expected from a computer system, since there are difficult semantics involved. (Onomastics, the study of the history of proper names such as toponyms is an entire discipline in the humanities.)

For quality assurance, one could involve a human to verify the output of our algorithm. Since this process costs the valuable time of an expert, it should be efficient in terms of user interaction – in particular, we do not want to require the user to carefully inspect all assigned places. Rather, the system should present parts of the solution that most require manual inspection. For these, it should in addition present alternatives

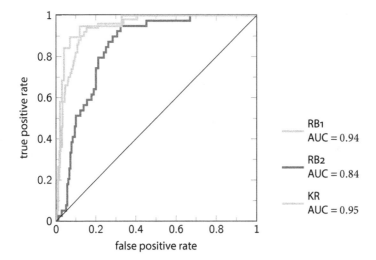

RB1
AUC = 0.94

RB2
AUC = 0.84

KR
AUC = 0.95

Figure 6.7: ROC curves for our classification on the three itinerary data sets, using best parameter values and GeoNames gazetteers.

that (hopefully) include the correct solution. We achieve both goals through sensitivity analysis, which can be computed efficiently (see Section 6.4.4).

6.7.1 Classification

Based on the sensitivity values for each assigned place, we consider the following classifier to decide which assignments warrant user inspection – that is, whether there is a good chance that the assignment might be wrong. Sort the places in the solution according to their sensitivity in increasing order, then classify all places with sensitivity values larger than θ as INSPECT, and all others as ASSUME CORRECT, for some parameter θ. (Alternatively, one can choose the threshold to be a rank rather than a value, as we did in Chapter 4.)

Our goal is for the user to be presented with most errors, while having to look at only relatively few places. We evaluate this classifier using receiver operating characteristic (ROC) curves: see Figure 6.7. The area under the curve (AUC) values in our experiments are 0.94 for RB1, 0.84 for RB2, and 0.95 for KR, all using GeoNames gazetteers. In general, AUC values between 0.8 and 0.9 can be considered excellent, while values over 0.9 are outstanding [HJL04]. In our specific case, this means that the classifier reliably discriminates between correct and incorrect assignments.

The classifier above allows us to put the user's attention on assignments that might be wrong. The next question is how to support the user in finding the correct assignment. The sensitivity analysis yields not only scores for the assigned places, but also for all other places. For a stop with an doubtful place assignment (identified as INSPECT by the

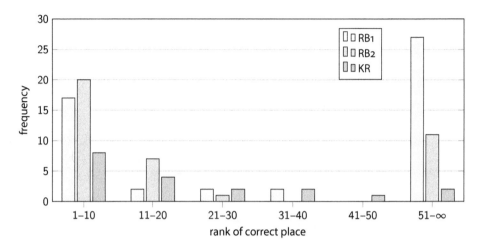

Figure 6.8: Rank of the correct place in the list of alternatives, ordered by descending Viterbi values. The histogram only contains the cases in which the place assigned by our algorithm is wrong (using GeoNames gazetteers and the parameters from Table 6.3).

classifier above), we use this information to select likely alternatives (in descending order of Viterbi value).

Based on our ground truth, we have evaluated at which rank in this sequence of alternatives the actual correct place is located. For all three itinerary data sets, using GeoNames gazetteers, we find that a considerable fraction of the correct places lies within the first 20 alternatives (see Figure 6.8). This means that we can present the user with a relatively small set of alternatives and expect the correct solution to be among them. For RB1, 91.2% of the places are either correctly assigned or within the first 20 alternatives; for the remaining two data sets, the number is similar. This shows that our user interaction can indeed significantly improve the overall accuracy.

6.7.2 User Interface

The classifier and the selection of alternatives described above are suitable for powering a graphical user interface. For instance, we can use color coding to visually draw the user's attention to places with high sensitivity. Figure 6.9 shows an itinerary from RB1: the color of the stops corresponds to sensitivity values from highly sensitive (red) to fairly robust (green). Indeed, four of the six stops colored in red are incorrect: Hlina[11], Schafhof, Schönberg, and Frankfurt.[12] There are no other errors in this solution, so having inspected only six out of 18 stops the user would have found all errors.

---

[11] The toponym in the itinerary corresponds to Schlan, which is the German name of the Czech town Slaný. However, this alternative spelling is not present in $\mathcal{G}$.

[12] The gazetteer contains two entries called Frankfurt, very near to each other, and the algorithm happened to choose the wrong one.

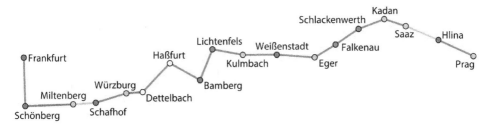

Figure 6.9: Solution to a Prague–Frankfurt itinerary from RB1, color-coded based on sensitivity values.

The line segments connecting the stops are also color-coded: here the color refers to the distance term $\mathbb{P}_d(\,\mathbf{P}_i\,|\,\mathbf{P}_{i-1}, \mathbf{D}_i\,)$ given by Equation (6.3). This presentation helps the user to assess whether the distances between the assigned places are plausible: if they are displayed in red, either the assignment is wrong or the distance given in the itinerary is particularly imprecise – either of which is potentially interesting.

In addition we can present a set of alternatives for any stop, for example on click or mouse-over. As was demonstrated in Sections 6.4 and 6.5, our algorithms are fast enough to support real-time interactions like this.

6.8 Concluding Remarks

We have taken a problem from the digital (geo-)humanities, formulated it properly as an optimization problem, and developed an efficient way of solving it – both asymptotically and in practice. We have shown experimentally that our algorithm outperforms the state of the art on this problem, both in accuracy and runtime. Our proper modeling enables automatic sensitivity analysis and we show that this forms a good basis for an algorithmically-supported user interface.

Some ideas for future work have been addressed throughout the text; here, we mention some additional directions. Blank and Henrich [BH16a] filter routes based on angles (rather than bearings). Our model could handle this by using a higher-order HMM, but then a straightforward application of the Viterbi algorithm takes $\Theta(kn^3)$ time. This would require improvement to be of practical value. In the context of user interactions, it would be interesting to develop a comprehensive graphical user interface for our system. This does not only include a properly designed-through version of the user interaction described in Section 6.7, but also possible user interactions for selecting gazetteer bounding boxes and itinerary bearings.

Another direction for future work is the following. The solution returned by our algorithm is not only useful for determining the spatial position of the given itinerary. For example, the calculated correspondences between modern and historical toponyms can also be used to enrich historical gazetteers. Improved gazetteers can in turn serve as a training set for the string similarity measure used in our approach.

We conclude this chapter with Figure 6.10, which shows 35 pages of the *Raißbüchlin* and our computed solutions on the 21 contained itineraries (RB1). This network, with 354 stops spanning a considerable part of Central Europe, was computed in about two minutes total runtime by the bidirectional lazy algorithm and has an accuracy of 85.9%.

Acknowledgments

We thank Daniel Blank for providing RB2 and Winfried Höhn for applying his work-in-progress OCR system to the *Raißbüchlin*. The research presented in this chapter was partially supported by the German Research Foundation (DFG), grant number Di 2161/2-1.

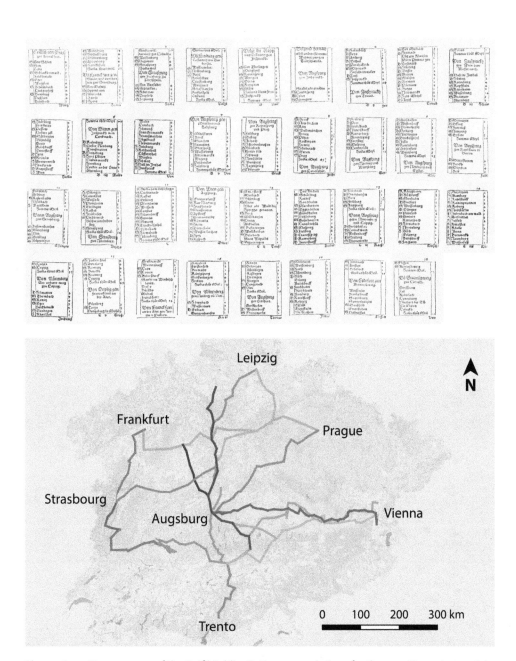

Figure 6.10: *Top:* 35 pages of the *Raißbüchlin*. *Bottom:* our solutions for those 21 itineraries, containing 354 stops and spanning a considerable part of Central Europe. It took two minutes to calculate these solutions.

Chapter 7

Conclusion

In this book, we have studied several problems arising in the context of information extraction from historical spatial documents. We give a short overview of our main contributions below. Additionally, we point to open research problems and make concrete proposals on how the algorithms and systems presented in this book can be extended in future work.

Locating Map Elements

In Chapter 3, we have presented a system for locating elements in historical maps. Our system combines template matching with active learning, which is used to derive a threshold that discriminates well between correct and incorrect matches. Subsequently, we have shown in experiments on six historical maps and in a user study that our system is accurate and efficient in utilizing user effort.

In the proof-of-concept implementation described in this book, we have used a fairly basic template matching algorithm. However, there are many more template matching algorithms described in the literature that could be used in our framework. Using a scale and rotation-invariant template matching algorithm (for example the algorithm by Kim and Alves de Araújo [KAdA07]) is likely to boost classification accuracy.

Proposal 1. Integrate an advanced template matching algorithm into our system.

We have addressed the problem of locating *basic* elements in historical maps. For subsequent steps in an information extraction process, it might be necessary to further combine the detected elements. In particular, it is desirable to locate text labels, while our approach only finds characters (or pre-defined words).

Proposal 2. Combine characters found with our approach to complete text labels.

The general problem of detecting text in historical maps has been discussed in the literature; however, it cannot be considered solved yet.

Open Problem 3. How to reliably locate text labels in historical maps?

We have shown that our approach for detecting elements is not limited to historical maps. When applied to incunables, the discrimination between correct and incorrect matches was in fact particularly clear, because these documents were printed with movable type (instead of being drawn by hand). Based on the resulting high detection accuracy, it might be possible to extend our technique to a full optical character recognition (OCR) system. Such an approach – optical character recognition on early prints using template matching – has also been advocated by Caluori and Simon [CS13a, CS13b].

Proposal 4. Build an OCR system for early prints based on our system.

Somewhat less ambitiously, the detected glyph occurrences can be used to quickly generate large amounts of synthetic training material. Our current implementation of the *Glyph Miner*[1] already supports typesetting arbitrary text using extracted glyphs. This kind of training data could be particularly useful for OCR systems that require large quantities of training data, such as systems based on deep learning. An example for an OCR system using deep learning is OCRopus [BUHAAS13].

Proposal 5. Use the *Glyph Miner* to generate synthetic training data for OCR.

In the description of our system, we assumed that the interaction with the user occurs in a single, continuous session. Once this session is finished, we determine a threshold for the template matches based on the user-provided information. This assumption can be considered an unnecessary restriction: new information can trivially be added to the underlying logistic regression model at any point, potentially leading to a better threshold. It is therefore of interest to enable the user to add additional information at a later time as well, even if a tentative threshold has already been determined.

This raises several questions in terms of user interaction, for example: how to communicate the impacts of a threshold change to the user? We could present the affected elements and ask the user to label them as correct or incorrect as well. This additional information, however, might lead to another threshold change when added to the model. It is unclear if this process converges quickly.

Open Problem 6. How to handle changes when integrating additional information once a threshold has been determined? What are appropriate user interactions?

Template matching is by no means the only technique from computer vision that requires the selection of a parameter: our active learning approach should be transferable to other computer vision problems.

Open Problem 7. How can active learning be applied for selecting parameters for other computer vision techniques?

Matching Markers and Labels

In Chapter 4, we have discussed an algorithm for matching place markers to their corresponding text labels. Our algorithm solves this problem efficiently and with high accuracy. We have shown that a related problem that can handle fragmented labels is NP-hard;

---

[1] `https://github.com/benedikt-budig/glyph-miner`

for a restricted version of this problem, we have given a polynomial-time algorithm. In addition, we have presented a prototype of a user interface that effectively points users towards uncertain marker-label assignments.

The prototype of our user interface is very primitive from a human-computer interaction point of view. In future work, the presented prototype could be extended into a comprehensive graphical user interface for our system. For example, the user experience would certainly benefit from a modern map presented next to the historical map for reference.

Proposal 8. Extend our prototype into a comprehensive graphical user interface.

In their current state, the presented user interactions are mainly aimed at expert users with knowledge of the local geography depicted on the map. It would be interesting to design smaller and simpler interactions so that volunteers are able to participate, for example on a crowdsourcing platform.

Open Problem 9. How can the marker-label matching task be transformed to suit crowdsourcing? More generally, what are appropriate design patterns for a crowdsourcing user interface?

Our algorithm performs a sensitivity analysis that identifies which assignments are uncertain. Once additional information is provided by the user, we recompute these values based on the previous solution, which works well in practice. However, it is still open how to efficiently recompute the sensitivity values in worst case (other than starting from scratch).

Open Problem 10. How to recompute sensitivity values more efficiently in worst case?

We have shown that a variant of our model that is able to handle label fragments is NP-hard. For a restricted case of the problem, we have given an efficient algorithm. However, it is also possible to develop heuristics that deal with the unrestricted problem sufficiently well in practice (see also Yu et al. [YLC16]). One might even be able to avoid handling fragments in this module altogether (see also Proposal 2).

Open Problem 11. How to handle label fragments algorithmically?

Another approach to handle label fragments is to design a user interaction in which a user provides information on the correct assignment of an ambiguous label fragment. This information can then be propagated in order to automatically assign other label fragments.

Open Problem 12. How to design a user interaction for handling label fragments? How to propagate information from user answers?

Extracting Building Footprints

In Chapter 5, we have dealt with the problem of extracting building footprints through a crowdsourcing pipeline that is run by the New York Public Library (NYPL). We have presented and experimentally evaluated an algorithm that improves the data quality for one of the pipeline steps: aggregating a group of user-contributed polygons into one consensus polygon. Using our method, the quality of the resulting polygons was significantly improved over that of the individual input polygons – without requiring additional user effort.

Our formulation of polygon consensus is based on a heuristic algorithm. In future work, it would be interesting to develop a formulation of polygon consensus as an optimization problem.

Open Problem 13. How to formulate polygon consensus as an optimization problem?

The current production version of the crowdsourcing pipeline uses a filtering step (see Section 5.3.4) to remove possible outliers. This step is based on clustering polygons in terms of their centroids, and the required distance threshold lacks a clear interpretation. It is desirable to replace this step with a model that is more convincing; possibly based on GDBSCAN [SEKX98] and the area of intersection between the polygons.

Open Problem 14. How to remove outliers from groups of user-contributed polygons in a theoretically-convincing way?

We have experimentally shown that groups that are *divisive* (that is, contain large numbers of outliers) have a strong negative impact on one variant of our algorithm, the parameter-free Auto-ε algorithm. Instead of (or in addition to) removing outliers in preprocessing, it might be possible to make the Auto-ε algorithm robust against such inputs.

Open Problem 15. How to make the Auto-ε algorithm robust against divisive groups?

After determining a consensus polygon, its accuracy can be further improved by taking the map image back into account. We have sketched in Section 5.4.4 how applying a local search strategy – starting from the consensus polygons towards areas with dark ink on the images – could be beneficial for geometric precision.

Proposal 16. Use the map image to improve the geometric precision of the consensus polygons. More specifically, combine local search with a user interface.

Apart from improving the polygon consensus step, future work could also address other steps in the information extraction process. Recall that the pipeline run by the NYPL starts with an image processing step that is supposed to detect the outlines of building footprints. The current implementation of this step [GA13] seems rather ad-hoc and could be replaced by more advanced image processing techniques to obtain better recognition results.

Open Problem 17. How to improve image processing for detecting building footprints?

Georeferencing Itineraries

In Chapter 6, we have presented a system for georeferencing historical itineraries. It combines textual and spatial information into a probabilistic model to deal with uncertainties inherent to historical itineraries. Our approach is able to solve this georeferencing problem efficiently and outperforms the state of the art in accuracy and runtime.

We have presented a prototype for an efficient user interaction based on sensitivity analysis. A user interface supporting this interaction should be created and evaluated in a user study with the target audience, that is, researchers from the humanities.

Proposal 18. Implement a graphical user interface based on Section 6.7 and evaluate it in a user study.

For our case study with the *Raißbüchlin*, we had to preform some amount of manual preprocessing on the toponyms (see Section 6.6). This is not desirable, but was necessary to normalize the toponyms from our various sources (the historical guidebook, the gazetteers, and the training data for the string similarity measure). This preprocessing step should be automated and put on proper theoretical foundation, preferably backed by expertise from the humanities. Improvements here would certainly benefit the practical applicability of our approach.

Open Problem 19. How to handle toponyms, respecting scientific insights from the humanities?

A competing approach by Blank and Henrich [BH16a] uses local angles instead of a global bearing. Transforming our model to reflect this behavior is straight-forward, but would increase the runtime from $O(kn^2)$ to $\Theta(kn^3)$.

Open Problem 20. How to integrate an assessment of local angles in less than $O(kn^3)$ time?

The presented approach handles each itinerary from a historical guidebook separately. It would be interesting to investigate if its accuracy could be increased by processing multiple itineraries at the same time, and to find a formulation for this problem that can still be solved efficiently.

Open Problem 21. Can the accuracy be increased by processing multiple itineraries simultaneously? How can we do this efficiently?

It might also be possible to transfer our approach to historical maps: the toponyms can be read from the text labels and the distances between place markers can be interpreted as the travel distances in our framework. However, it is unclear if our modeling can be modified such that it can still be solve in polynomial time.

Open Problem 22. How can we adapt our probabilistic framework to maps and efficiently find solutions?

Outlook

In this book, we have developed four different modules addressing information extraction tasks from historical spatial documents. These modules can serve as a starting point for composing various extraction pipelines. Particularly useful would be a module that is able to read previously identified text labels and perform reliable optical character recognition. Although there is some recent development in this direction (for example by Höhn [Höh17]), to the best of our knowledge, the problem cannot considered to be solved.[2]

Open Problem 23. How to do optical character recognition for text on historical maps?

There are many more information extraction challenges in historical spatial documents that are not solved yet. This includes for example the detection of rivers, political borders, forest areas, and road networks. These challenges should be addressed using our methodology, creating interchangeable modules together with clear evaluation criteria.

Because of the multiplicity of historical spatial documents and the different challenges they impose, we doubt that a single pipeline will be able to successfully process all of these documents. Instead, the individual character of each historical document (or corpus) might require a different set of modules: together, these modules form a custom information extraction process. Thus, the common goal for future work should be to develop a collection of modules with interfaces that fit together, in the sense of a toolbox of lean, seamlessly integrated tools with clearly defined objectives.

---

[2] It has certainly not been solved *in practice* yet. Consider for example the recently started crowdsourcing project by Southall et al. [SAF+17], in which millions of place names from British Ordnance Survey maps are manually transcribed by volunteers. These maps were created between 1888 and 1914, with high and consistent production standards. Still, the authors explicitly state that – in their opinion – manual transcription is "currently the only feasible way to gather large amounts of textual [...] place data" from these historical maps.

Bibliography

[ABKS99] Mihael Ankerst, Markus M. Breunig, Hans-Peter Kriegel, and Jörg Sander. OPTICS: Ordering Points to Identify the Clustering Structure. In *Proceedings of the 1999 ACM SIGMOD International Conference on Management of Data (SIGMOD '99)*, pages 49–60. ACM, 1999.

[Ahl13] Dirk Ahlers. Assessment of the Accuracy of GeoNames Gazetteer Data. In *Proceedings of the 7th Workshop on Geographic Information Retrieval (GIR '13)*, pages 74–81. ACM, 2013.

[Ano97] Anonymous. *Kronn und Auszbunde aller Wegweiser*. Published by Lambertus Andree, Köln, 1597. Source: Austrian National Library, available online at http://data.onb.ac.at/rec/AC10037959.

[ARTL15] David Aldavert, Marçal Rusiñol, Ricardo Toledo, and Josep Lladós. A study of Bag-of-Visual-Words representations for handwritten keyword spotting. *International Journal on Document Analysis and Recognition (IJDAR)*, 18(3):223–234, 2015.

[AS14] Marco D. Adelfio and Hanan Samet. Itinerary Retrieval: Travelers, Like Traveling Salesmen, Prefer Efficient Routes. In *Proceedings of the 8th Workshop on Geographic Information Retrieval (GIR '14)*, pages 1:1–1:8. ACM, 2014.

[AZMH15] Jamal Jokar Arsanjani, Alexander Zipf, Peter Mooney, and Marco Helbich. *OpenStreetMap in GIScience: Experiences, Research, and Applications*. Springer, 2015.

[BAU07] Victor Bucha, Sergey Ablameyko, and Seiichi Uchida. Image Pixel Force Fields and their Application for Color Map Vectorisation. In *Proceedings of the 9th International Conference on Document Analysis and Recognition (ICDAR 2007)*, pages 1228–1242. IEEE, 2007.

[BBvK+13] Kevin Buchin, Maike Buchin, Marc van Kreveld, Maarten Löffler, Rodrigo I. Silveira, Carola Wenk, and Lionov Wiratma. Median Trajectories. *Algorithmica*, 66(3):595–614, 2013.

[BCJR74] Lalit Bahl, John Cocke, Frederick Jelinek, and Josef Raviv. Optimal decoding of linear codes for minimizing symbol error rate. *IEEE Transactions on Information Theory*, 20(2):284–287, 1974.

Bibliography

[BDTG17] James O. Butler, Christopher E. Donaldson, Joanna E. Taylor, and Ian N. Gregory. Alts, Abbreviations, and AKAs: Historical Onomastic Variation and Automated Named Entity Recognition. *Journal of Map & Geography Libraries*, 13(1):58–81, 2017.

[Beh14] Martin Behr. *Buchdruck und Sprachwandel*. De Gruyter, 2014.

[BGG⁺16] Caterina Balletti, Ludovica Galeazzo, Caterina Gottardi, Francesco Guerra, and Paolo Vernier. New technologies applied to the history of the Venice Lagoon. In *Proceedings of the 11th ICA Conference Digital Approaches to Cartographic Heritage*, pages 182–190. AUTH, 2016.

[BH15] Daniel Blank and Andreas Henrich. Geocoding Place Names from Historic Route Descriptions. In *Proceedings of the 9th Workshop on Geographic Information Retrieval (GIR '15)*, pages 9:1–9:2. ACM, 2015.

[BH16a] Daniel Blank and Andreas Henrich. A Depth-first Branch-and-bound Algorithm for Geocoding Historic Itinerary Tables. In *Proceedings of the 10th Workshop on Geographic Information Retrieval (GIR '16)*, pages 3:1–3:10. ACM, 2016.

[BH16b] Daniel Blank and Andreas Henrich. Die computergestützte Erschließung und Visualisierung historischer Itinerare. In *Conference Abstracts of the 3. Tagung des Verbands Digital Humanities im deutschsprachigen Raum (DHd '16)*, pages 277–281, 2016.

[BKW15] Ralf Bill, Nils Koldrack, and Kai Walter. Georeferenzierung alter topographischer Karten – Crowdsourcing versus Bildverarbeitung. *AGIT. Journal für Angewandte Geoinformatik*, 1-2015:540–549, 2015.

[BMS16] Merrick Lex Berman, Ruth Mostern, and Humphrey Southall, editors. *Placing Names: Enriching and Integrating Gazetteers*. Indiana University Press, 2016.

[BNG⁺06] Brent Bryan, Robert C. Nichol, Christopher R Genovese, Jeff Schneider, Christopher J. Miller, and Larry Wasserman. Active Learning for Identifying Function Threshold Boundaries. In *Advances in Neural Information Processing Systems 18 (NIPS '05)*, pages 163–170. MIT Press, 2006.

[Bre08] Thomas M. Breuel. The OCRopus Open Source OCR System. In Berrin A. Yanikoglou and Kathrin Berkner, editors, *Document Recogntion and Retrival XV*, volume 6815. SPIE, 2008.

[Bru09] Roberto Brunelli. *Template Matching Techniques in Computer Vision: Theory and Practice*. John Wiley & Sons, 2009.

[BUHAAS13] Thomas M. Breuel, Adnan Ul-Hasan, Mayce Ali Al-Azawi, and Faisal Shafait. High-Performance OCR for Printed English and Fraktur Using LSTM Networks. In *Proceedings of the 12th International Conference on Document Analysis and Recognition (ICDAR '13)*, pages 683–687. IEEE, 2013.

[BV04] Stephen Boyd and Lieven Vandenberghe. *Convex Optimization*. Cambridge University Press, 2004.

[BvD15] Benedikt Budig and Thomas C. van Dijk. Active Learning for Classifying Template Matches in Historical Maps. In *Proceedings of the 18th International Conference on Discovery Science (DS '15)*, volume 9356 of *LNCS*, pages 33–47. Springer, 2015.

[BvD17] Benedikt Budig and Thomas C. van Dijk. Journeys of the Past: A Hidden Markov Approach to Georeferencing Historical Itineraries. In *Proceedings of the 11th Workshop on Geographic Information Retrieval (GIR '17)*, 2017.

[BvDFA16] Benedikt Budig, Thomas C. van Dijk, Fabian Feitsch, and Mauricio Giraldo Arteaga. Polygon Consensus: Smart Crowdsourcing for Extracting Building Footprints from Historical Maps. In *Proceedings of the 24th ACM SIGSPATIAL International Conference on Advances in Geographic Information Systems (ACM SIGSPATIAL '16)*, pages 66:1–66:4. ACM, 2016.

[BvDK16] Benedikt Budig, Thomas C. van Dijk, and Felix Kirchner. Glyph Miner: A System for Efficiently Extracting Glyphs from Early Prints in the Context of OCR. In *Proceedings of the 16th ACM/IEEE-CS Joint Conference on Digital Libraries (JCDL '16)*, pages 31–34. ACM, 2016.

[BvDW14] Benedikt Budig, Thomas C. van Dijk, and Alexander Wolff. Matching Labels and Markers in Historical Maps: an Algorithm with Interactive Postprocessing. In *Proceedings of the 2nd ACM SIGSPATIAL International Workshop on MapInteraction (MapInteract '14)*, pages 22–28. ACM, 2014.

[BvDW16] Benedikt Budig, Thomas C. van Dijk, and Alexander Wolff. Matching Labels and Markers in Historical Maps: An Algorithm with Interactive Postprocessing. *ACM Transactions on Spatial Algorithms and Systems (TSAS)*, 2(4):13:1–13:24, 2016.

[BWM14] Ralf Bill, Kai Walter, and Jacob Mendt. Virtuelles Kartenforum 2.0 – Verfügbarmachung von Altkarten über eine räumliche Portalanwendung. In Josef Strobl, Thomas Blaschke, Gerald Griesebner, and Bernhard Zagel, editors, *Angewandte Geoinformatik 2014: Beiträge zum 26. AGIT-Symposium Salzburg*, 2014.

Bibliography

[Chi15] Yao-Yi Chiang. Querying Historical Maps as a Unified, Structured, and Linked Spatiotemporal Source. In *Proceedings of the 23rd ACM SIGSPATIAL International Conference on Advances in Geographic Information Systems (ACM SIGSPATIAL '15)*, pages 270–273. ACM, 2015.

[CK11] Yao-Yi Chiang and Craig A. Knoblock. Recognition of Multi-Oriented, Multi-Sized, and Curved Text. In *Proceedings of the 11th International Conference on Document Analysis and Recognition (ICDAR '11)*, pages 1399–1403. IEEE, 2011.

[CK13a] Yuxin Chen and Andreas Krause. Near-Optimal Batch Mode Active Learning and Adaptive Submodular Optimization. In *Proceedings of the 30th International Conference on Machine Learning (ICML '13)*, pages 160–168. JMLR, 2013.

[CK13b] Yao-Yi Chiang and Craig A. Knoblock. A general approach for extracting road vector data from raster maps. *International Journal on Document Analysis and Recognition (IJDAR)*, 16(1):55–81, 2013.

[CK15] Yao-Yi Chiang and Craig A. Knoblock. Recognizing text in raster maps. *GeoInformatica*, 19(1):1–27, 2015.

[CLHN+16] Yao-Yi Chiang, Stefan Leyk, Narges Honarvar Nazari, Sima Moghaddam, and Tian Xiang Tan. Assessing the Impact of Graphical Quality on Automatic Text Recognition in Digital Maps. *Computers & Geosciences*, 93:21–35, 2016.

[CLK14] Yao-Yi Chiang, Stefan Leyk, and Craig A. Knoblock. A Survey of Digital Map Processing Techniques. *ACM Computing Surveys (CSUR)*, 47(1):1:1–1:44, 2014.

[CLRS09] Thomas H. Cormen, Charles E. Leiserson, Ronald L. Rivest, and Clifford Stein. *Introduction to Algorithms*. MIT Press, 3rd edition, 2009.

[CS13a] Ursina Caluori and Klaus Simon. Glyph Recognition by Pattern Matching with On-the-fly Generated Patterns. In *Proceedings of the 21st International Conference on Software, Telecommunications and Computer Networks (SoftCOM '13)*, pages 1–5. IEEE, 2013.

[CS13b] Ursina Caluori and Klaus Simon. An OCR Concept for Historic Prints. In *Proceedings of the 2013 IS&T Archiving Conference*, pages 143–147. IS&T, 2013.

[dBKS+01] Rolf A. de By, Richard A. Knippers, Yuxian Sun, Martin C. Ellis, Menno-Jan Kraak, Michael J. C. Weir, Yola Georgiadou, Mostafa M. Radwan, Cees J. van Westen, Wolfgang Kainz, and Edmund J. Sides. *Principles of Geographic Information Systems: An Introductory Textbook*. ITC, 2001.

[DC06] Deeptendu Bikash Dhar and Bhabatosh Chanda. Extraction and recognition of geographical features from paper maps. *International Journal of Document Analysis and Recognition (IJDAR)*, 8(4):232–245, 2006.

[DC08] Pinar Donmez and Jaime G. Carbonell. Proactive Learning: Cost-Sensitive Active Learning with Multiple Imperfect Oracles. In *Proceedings of the 17th ACM Conference on Information and Knowledge Management (CIKM '08)*, pages 619–628. ACM, 2008.

[DLCKP+14] Livio De La Cruz, Stephen Kobourov, Sergey Pupyrev, Paul S. Shen, and Sankar Veeramoni. Computing Consensus Curves. In *Proceedings of the 13th International Symposium on Experimental Algorithms (SEA '14)*, volume 8504 of *LNCS*, pages 223–234. Springer, 2014.

[DLMS95] Marc Pierrot Deseilligny, Hervé Le Men, and Georges Stamon. Character String Recognition on Maps, a Rotation-invariant Recognition Method. *Pattern Recognition Letters*, 16(12):1297–1310, 1995.

[DM98] Leonardo Dagum and Ramesh Menon. OpenMP: An Industry-Standard API for Shared-Memory Programming. *IEEE Computational Science & Engineering*, 5(1):46–55, 1998.

[Edm65] Jack Edmonds. Paths, Trees, and Flowers. *Canadian Journal of Mathematics*, 17(3):449–467, 1965.

[EGF07] Andrea Ernst-Gerlach and Norbert Fuhr. Retrieval in Text Collections with Historic Spelling Using Linguistic and Spelling Variants. In *Proceedings of the 7th ACM/IEEE-CS Joint Conference on Digital Libraries (JCDL '07)*, pages 333–341. ACM, 2007.

[EKSX96] Martin Ester, Hans-Peter Kriegel, Jörg Sander, and Xiaowei Xu. A Density-Based Algorithm for Discovering Clusters in Large Spatial Databases with Noise. In *Proceedings of the 2nd International Conference on Knowledge Discovery and Data Mining (KDD-96)*, pages 226–231. AAAI Press, 1996.

[EOW10] Boris Epshtein, Eyal Ofek, and Yonatan Wexler. Detecting Text in Natural Scenes with Stroke Width Transform. In *Proceedings of the 2010 IEEE Conference on Computer Vision and Pattern Recognition (CVPR '10)*, pages 2963–2970. IEEE, 2010.

[FAFF02] Jon Feldman, Ibrahim Abou-Faycal, and Matteo Frigo. A Fast Maximum-Likelihood Decoder for Convolutional Codes. In *Proceedings of the 56th IEEE Vehicular Technology Conference*, volume 1, pages 371–375. IEEE, 2002.

[Faw06] Tom Fawcett. An introduction to ROC analysis. *Pattern Recognition Letters*, 27(8):861–874, 2006.

Bibliography

[FKP12] Christopher Fleet, Kimberly C. Kowal, and Petr Přidal. Georeferencer: Crowdsourced Georeferencing for Map Library Collections. *D-Lib Magazine*, 18(11/12), 2012.

[FvR09] Wolf-Armin Freiherr von Reitzenstein. *Lexikon fränkischer Ortsnamen: Herkunft und Bedeutung. Oberfranken, Mittelfranken, Unterfranken.* C.H. Beck, München, 2009.

[FvR13] Wolf-Armin Freiherr von Reitzenstein. *Lexikon bayerischer Ortsnamen: Herkunft und Bedeutung. Oberbayern, Niederbayern, Oberpfalz.* C.H. Beck, München, 2013.

[GA13] Mauricio Giraldo Arteaga. Historical Map Polygon and Feature Extractor. In *Proceedings of the 1st ACM SIGSPATIAL International Workshop on MapInteraction (MapInteract '13)*, pages 66–71. ACM, 2013.

[Gol97] Andrew V. Goldberg. An Efficient Implementation of a Scaling Minimum-Cost Flow Algorithm. *Journal of Algorithms*, 22:1–29, 1997.

[Goo07] Michael F. Goodchild. Citizens as sensors: the world of volunteered geography. *GeoJournal*, 69(4):211–221, 2007.

[GS08] Yuhong Guo and Dale Schuurmans. Discriminative Batch Mode Active Learning. In *Advances in Neural Information Processing Systems 20 (NIPS '07)*, pages 593–600. MIT Press, 2008.

[GT88] Andrew V. Goldberg and Robert E. Tarjan. A New Approach to the Maximum-flow Problem. *Journal of the ACM*, 35(4):921–940, 1988.

[GT89] Andrew V. Goldberg and Robert E. Tarjan. Finding Minimum-cost Circulations by Canceling Negative Cycles. *Journal of the ACM*, 36(4):873–886, 1989.

[GWL15] Björn Gottfried, Marius Wegner, and Mathias Lawo. Towards the interactive transcription of handwritings: anytime anywhere document analysis. *International Journal on Document Analysis and Recognition (IJDAR)*, 18(1):31–45, 2015.

[Hak10] Mordechai Haklay. How good is volunteered geographical information? A comparative study of OpenStreetMap and Ordnance Survey datasets. *Environment and Planning B: Planning and Design*, 37(4):682–703, 2010.

[HBH+03] Hermann V. Hilprecht, Immanuel Benzinger, Fritz Hommel, Peter C. A. Jensen, and Georg Steindorff. *Explorations in Bible Lands During the 19th Century.* A.J. Holman, 1903.

[HHC93] Yunghsiang S. Han, Carlos R. P. Hartmann, and Chih-Chieh Chen. Efficient Priority-First Search Maximum-Likelihood Soft-Decision Decoding of Linear Block Codes. *IEEE Transactions on Information Theory*, 39(5):1514–1523, 1993.

[HJL04] David W. Hosmer Jr. and Stanley Lemeshow. *Applied Logistic Regression*. John Wiley & Sons, 2004.

[HJZL06] Steven Hoi, Rong Jin, Jianke Zhu, and Michael Lyu. Batch Mode Active Learning and Its Application to Medical Image Classification. In *Proceedings of the 23rd International Conference on Machine Learning (ICML '06)*, pages 417–424. JMLR, 2006.

[HK73] John E. Hopcroft and Richard M. Karp. An $n^{5/2}$ algorithm for maximal matchings in bipartite graphs. *SIAM Journal on Computing*, 2(4):225–231, 1973.

[HKKM14] Andreas Hackeloeer, Klaas Klasing, Jukka M. Krisp, and Liqiu Meng. Georeferencing: a review of methods and applications. *Annals of GIS*, 20(1):61–69, 2014.

[HKN+17] Hendrik Herold, Helen Kollai, Marco Neubert, Gotthard Meinel, Richard Gruntzke, and Peter Winkler. Metadata-Aware Map Processing. In *Proceedings of the 2nd Workshop on Exploring Old Maps (EOM '17)*, pages 13–14, 2017.

[HL09] Thomas C. Henderson and Trevor Linton. Raster Map Image Analysis. In *Proceedings of the 10th International Conference on Document Analysis and Recognition (ICDAR '09)*, pages 376–380. IEEE, 2009.

[Höh13] Winfried Höhn. Detecting Arbitrarily Oriented Text Labels in Early Maps. In *Proceedings of the 6th Iberian Conference on Pattern Recognition and Image Analysis (IbPRIA '13)*, volume 7887 of *LNCS*, pages 424–432. Springer, 2013.

[Höh17] Winfried Höhn. Deep Learning for Place Name OCR in Early Maps. In *Proceedings of the 2nd Workshop on Exploring Old Maps (EOM '17)*, pages 17–18, 2017.

[Hol13] Andreas Holzinger. Human-Computer Interaction and Knowledge Discovery (HCI-KDD): What Is the Benefit of Bringing Those Two Fields to Work Together? In Alfredo Cuzzocrea, Christian Kittl, Dimitris E. Simos, Edgar Weippl, and Lida Xu, editors, *Availability, Reliability, and Security in Information Systems and HCI*, pages 319–328. Springer, 2013.

[HRLG13] Bernhard Haslhofer, Werner Robitza, Carl Lagoze, and Francois Guimbretiere. Semantic Tagging on Historical Maps. In *Proceedings of the 5th*

Bibliography

Annual ACM Web Science Conference (WebSci '13), pages 148–157. ACM, 2013.

[HS17a] Winfried Höhn and Christoph Schommer. Georeferencing of Place Markers in Digitized Early Maps by Using Similar Maps as Data Source. In *Digital Humanities 2017: Conference Abstracts*, pages 473–475, 2017.

[HS17b] Winfried Höhn and Christoph Schommer. RAT 2.0. In *Digital Humanities 2017: Conference Abstracts*, pages 472–473, 2017.

[HSS13] Winfried Höhn, Hans-Günter Schmidt, and Hendrik Schöneberg. Semi-automatic Recognition and Georeferencing of Places in Early Maps. In *Proceedings of the 13th ACM/IEEE-CS Joint Conference on Digital Libraries (JCDL '13)*, pages 335–338. ACM, 2013.

[HW08] Mordechai Haklay and Patrick Weber. OpenStreetMap: User-Generated Street Maps. *IEEE Pervasive Computing*, 7(4):12–18, 2008.

[ITH16] Ionuț Iosifescu, Angeliki Tsorlini, and Lorenz Hurni. Towards a comprehensive methodology for automatic vectorization of raster historical maps. *e-Perimetron*, 11(2):57–76, 2016.

[Jac12] Paul Jaccard. The Distribution of the Flora in the Alpine Zone. *New Phytologist*, 11(2):37–50, 1912.

[JH11] Bernhard Jenny and Lorenz Hurni. Studying Cartographic Heritage: Analysis and Visualization of Geometric Distortions. *Computers & Graphics*, 35(2):402–411, 2011.

[Job10] Markus Jobst, editor. *Preservation in Digital Cartography: Archiving Aspects*. LNG&C. Springer, 2010.

[JSPH12] Krzysztof Janowicz, Simon Scheider, Todd Pehle, and Glen Hart. Geospatial Semantics and Linked Spatiotemporal Data – Past, Present, and Future. *Semantic Web*, 3(4):321–332, 2012.

[KAdA07] Hae Yong Kim and Sidnei Alves de Araújo. Grayscale Template-Matching Invariant to Rotation, Scale, Translation, Brightness and Contrast. In Domingo Mery and Luis Rueda, editors, *Advances in Image and Video Technology: Proceedings of the 2nd Pacific Rim Symposium on Image and Video Technology (PSIVT '07)*, volume 4872 of *LNCS*, pages 100–113. Springer, 2007.

[Kar72] Richard M. Karp. Reducibility Among Combinatorial Problems. In Raymond E. Miller, James W. Thatcher, and Jean D. Bohlinger, editors, *Proceedings of a symposium on the Complexity of Computer Computations*, pages 85–103. Springer, 1972.

[Kar11] Richard M. Karp. Understanding Science Through the Computational Lens. *Journal of Computer Science and Technology*, 26(4):569–577, 2011.

[KDBN16] Felix Kirchner, Marco Dittrich, Phillip Beckenbauer, and Maximilian Nöth. OCR bei Inkunabeln – Offizinspezifischer Ansatz der Universitätsbibliothek Würzburg. *ABI Technik*, 36(3):178–188, 2016.

[Kıl16] Deniz Kılınç. An accurate toponym-matching measure based on approximate string matching. *Journal of Information Science*, 42(2):138–149, 2016.

[KKK⁺16] Dominik Kaim, Jacek Kozak, Natalia Kolecka, Elżbieta Ziółkowska, Krzysztof Ostafin, Katarzyna Ostapowicz, Urs Gimmi, Catalina Munteanu, and Volker C. Radeloff. Broad scale forest cover reconstruction from historical topographic maps. *Applied Geography*, 67:39–48, 2016.

[Knu13] Matthew Allen Knutzen. Unbinding the Atlas: Moving the NYPL Map Collection Beyond Digitization. *Journal of Map & Geography Libraries*, 9(1–2):8–24, 2013.

[Kra81] Samuel N. Kramer. *History begins at Sumer: Thirty-Nine Firsts in Man's Recorded History*. University of Pennsylvania Press, 3rd edition, 1981.

[Krü74] Herbert Krüger. *Das älteste deutsche Routenhandbuch. Jörg Gails „Raißbüchlin"*. Akademische Druck- und Verlagsanstalt Graz, 1974.

[KVW13] Arbaz Khan, Maria Vasardani, and Stephan Winter. Extracting Spatial Information From Place Descriptions. In *Proceedings of the 1st ACM SIGSPATIAL Int. Workshop on Computational Models of Place (COMP '13)*, pages 62:62–62:69. ACM, 2013.

[Lar09] Reif Larsen. *The Selected Works of T. S. Spivet*, page 138. Penguin Books, 2009.

[LB09] Stefan Leyk and Ruedi Boesch. Extracting Composite Cartographic Area Features in Low-Quality Maps. *Cartography and Geographic Information Science*, 36(1):71–79, 2009.

[LBLD11] Stephen D. Laycock, Philip G. Brown, Robert G. Laycock, and Andy M. Day. Aligning Archive Maps and Extracting Footprints for Analysis of Historic Urban Environments. *Computers & Graphics*, 35(2):242–249, 2011.

[LBW06] Stefan Leyk, Ruedi Boesch, and Robert Weibel. Saliency and semantic processing: Extracting forest cover from historical topographic maps. *Pattern Recognition*, 39(5):953–968, 2006.

[Lev66] Vladimir I. Levenshtein. Binary codes capable of correcting deletions, insertions, and reversals. *Soviet Physics Doklady*, 10(8):707–710, 1966.

Bibliography

[Ley10] Stefan Leyk. Segmentation of Colour Layers in Historical Maps Based on Hierarchical Colour Sampling. In Jean-Marc Ogier, Wenyin Liu, and Josep Lladós, editors, *Proceedings on the 8th International Workshop on Graphics Recognition (GREC '09)*, number 6020 in LNCS, pages 231–241. Springer, 2010.

[LGMR15] Paul A. Longley, Michael F. Goodchild, David J. Maguire, and David W. Rhind. *Geographic Information Systems and Science.* John Wiley & Sons, 4th edition, 2015.

[Liu02] Yuncai Liu. An automation system: generation of digital map data from pictorial map resources. *Pattern Recognition*, 35(9):1973–1987, 2002.

[Llo82] Stuart P. Lloyd. Least squares quantization in PCM. *IEEE Transactions on Information Theory*, 28(2):129–137, 1982.

[LS11] Lantao Liu and Dylan A. Shell. Assessing Optimal Assignment Under Uncertainty: An Interval-based Algorithm. *The International Journal of Robotics Research*, 30(7):936–953, 2011.

[LvA11] Edith Law and Luis von Ahn. Human computation. *Synthesis Lectures on Artificial Intelligence and Machine Learning*, 5(3):1–121, 2011.

[Mäh92] Hans-Joachim Mähl. Nachwort zu: *Sebastian Brant: Das Narrenschiff*, page 461. Reclam, 1992.

[MAHL13] Richard J. Marciano, Robert C. Allen, Chien-Yi Hou, and Pamella R. Lach. "Big Historical Data" Feature Extraction. *Journal of Map & Geography Libraries*, 9(1–2):69–80, 2013.

[MC09] Reza Farrahi Moghaddam and Mohamed Cheriet. Application of Multi-Level Classifiers and Clustering for Automatic Word Spotting in Historical Document Images. In *Proceedings of the 10th International Conference on Document Analysis and Recognition (ICDAR '09)*, pages 511–515. IEEE, 2009.

[MCdS12] Carlos A. B. Mello, Diogo C. Costa, and Tiago J. dos Santos. Automatic Image Segmentation of Old Topographic Maps and Floor Plans. In *Proceedings of the 2012 IEEE International Conference on Systems, Man, and Cybernetics (SMC '12)*, pages 132–137. IEEE, 2012.

[Meu07] Peter H. Meurer. Cartography in the German Lands, 1450–1650. In David Woodward, editor, *The History of Cartography*, volume 3, chapter 42, pages 1172–1245. University of Chicago Press, 2007.

[MGNIM16] Ludovic Moncla, Mauro Gaio, Javier Nogueras-Iso, and Sébastien Mustière. Reconstruction of itineraries from annotated text with an informed spanning tree algorithm. *International Journal of Geographical Information Science*, 30(6):1137–1160, 2016.

[MLK+04] Takaharu Miyoshi, Weiqing Li, Kazufumi Kaneda, Hideo Yamashita, and Eihachiro Nakamae. Automatic Extraction of Buildings Utilizing Geometric Features of a Scanned Topographic Map. In *Proceedings of the 17th International Conference on Pattern Recognition (ICPR '04)*, pages 626–629. IEEE, 2004.

[MM17] Fernando Melo and Bruno Martins. Automated Geocoding of Textual Documents: A Survey of Current Approaches. *Transactions in GIS*, 21(1):3–38, 2 2017.

[MRANG14] Ludovic Moncla, Walter Renteria-Agualimpia, Javier Nogueras-Iso, and Mauro Gaio. Geocoding for Texts with Fine-grain Toponyms: An Experiment on a Geoparsed Hiking Descriptions Corpus. In *Proceedings of the 22nd ACM SIGSPATIAL International Conference on Advances in Geographic Information Systems (ACM SIGSPATIAL '14)*, pages 183–192. ACM, 2014.

[NK09] Paul Newson and John Krumm. Hidden Markov Map Matching Through Noise and Sparseness. In *Proceedings of the 17th ACM SIGSPATIAL International Conference on Advances in Geographic Information Systems (ACM SIGSPATIAL '09)*, pages 336–343. ACM, 2009.

[NTC16] Narges Honarvar Nazari, Tianxiang Tan, and Yao-Yi Chiang. Integrating Text Recognition for Overlapping Text Detection in Maps. In *Proceedings of the 23rd Document Recognition and Retrieval Conference (DRR XXIII)*, pages 1–8. IS&T, 2016.

[OIK+17] Krzysztof Ostafin, Marcin Iwanowski, Jacek Kozak, Arkadiusz Cacko, Urs Gimmi, Dominik Kaim, Achilleas Psomas, Christian Ginzler, and Katarzyna Ostapowicz. Forest cover mask from historical topographic maps based on image processing. *Geoscience Data Journal*, 4(1):29–39, 2017.

[Par11] Charles Parker. An Analysis of Performance Measures For Binary Classifiers. In *Proceedings of the 11th International Conference on Data Mining (ICDM '11)*, pages 517–526. IEEE, 2011.

[Pea86] Judea Pearl. Fusion, Propagation, and Structuring in Belief Networks. *Artificial Intelligence*, 29(3):241–288, 1986.

Bibliography

[Pos69] Hans Joachim Postel. Die Kölner Phonetik. Ein Verfahren zur Identifizierung von Personennamen auf der Grundlage der Gestaltanalyse. *IBM-Nachrichten*, 19:925–931, 1969.

[PVG⁺11] Fabian Pedregosa, Gael Varoquaux, Alexandre Gramfort, Vincent Michel, Bertrand Thirion, Olivier Grisel, Mathieu Blondel, Peter Prettenhofer, Ron Weiss, Vincent Dubourg, Jake Vanderplas, Alexandre Passos, David Cournapeau, Matthieu Brucher, Matthieu Perrot, Edouard Duchesnay, and Gilles Louppe. Scikit-learn: Machine Learning in Python. *Journal of Machine Learning Research*, 12:2825–2830, 2011.

[RBO08] Romain Raveaux, Jean-Christophe Burie, and Jean-Marc Ogier. Object Extraction from Colour Cadastral Maps. In *Proceedings of the 8th IAPR International Workshop on Document Analysis Systems (DAS '08)*, pages 506–514. IEEE, 2008.

[Ris68] Walter W. Ristow. United States Fire Insurance and Underwriters Maps, 1852–1968. *The Quarterly Journal of the Library of Congress*, 25(3):194–218, 1968.

[RL13] Gabriel Recchia and Max Louwerse. A Comparison of String Similarity Measures for Toponym Matching. In *Proceedings of the 1st ACM SIGSPATIAL International Workshop on Computational Models of Place (COMP '13)*, pages 54–61. ACM, 2013.

[RM03] Toni M. Rath and Raghavan Manmatha. Word Image Matching Using Dynamic Time Warping. In *Proceedings of the IEEE Computer Society Conference on Computer Vision and Pattern Recognition (CVPR '03)*, volume 2, pages 521–527. IEEE, 2003.

[RM07] Toni M. Rath and Raghavan Manmatha. Word Spotting for Historical Documents. *International Journal of Document Analysis and Recognition (IJDAR)*, 9(2-4):139–152, 2007.

[RN09] Stuart Russell and Peter Norvig. *Artificial Intelligence: A Modern Approach*. Prentice Hall Press, 3rd edition, 2009.

[RPL14] Partha Pratim Roy, Umapada Pal, and Josep Lladós. Word searching in unconstrained layout using character pair coding. *International Journal on Document Analysis and Recognition (IJDAR)*, 17(4):343–358, 2014.

[RY98] Eric Sven Ristad and Peter N. Yianilos. Learning String-Edit Distance. *IEEE Transactions on Pattern Analysis and Machine Intelligence*, 20(5):522–532, 1998.

[SAF+17] Humphrey Southall, Paula Aucott, Chris Fleet, Tom Pert, and Michael Stoner. GB1900: Engaging the Public in Very Large Scale Gazetteer Construction from the Ordnance Survey "County Series" 1:10,560 Mapping of Great Britain. *Journal of Map & Geography Libraries*, 13(1):7–28, 2017.

[SB11] Tenzing Shaw and Peter Bajcsy. Automation of Digital Historical Map Analyses. In *Proceedings of the IS&T/SPIE Electronic Imaging 2011*, volume 7869. SPIE, 2011.

[SBI12] Rainer Simon, Elton Barker, and Leif Isaksen. Exploring Pelagios: A Visual Browser for Geo-Tagged Datasets. In Eneko Agirre, Kate Fernie, Arantxa Otegi, and Mark Stevenson, editors, *Proceedings of the International Workshop on Supporting Users' Exploration of Digital Libraries*, pages 29–34, 2012.

[SBIdSC15] Rainer Simon, Elton Barker, Leif Isaksen, and Pau de Soto Cañamares. Linking Early Geospatial Documents, One Place at a Time: Annotation of Geographic Documents with Recogito. *e-Perimetron*, 10(2):49–59, 2015.

[Sch03] Alexander Schrijver. *Combinatorial Optimization: Polyhedra and Efficiency*. Springer, 2003.

[SEKX98] Jörg Sander, Martin Ester, Hans-Peter Kriegel, and Xiaowei Xu. Density-Based Clustering in Spatial Databases: The Algorithm GDBSCAN and Its Applications. *Data Mining and Knowledge Discovery*, 2(2):169–194, 1998.

[Set10] Burr Settles. Active Learning Literature Survey. Computer Sciences Technical Report 1648, University of Wisconsin-Madison, 2010.

[Set12] Burr Settles. *Active Learning*. Synthesis Lectures on Artificial Intelligence and Machine Learning. Morgan & Claypool Publishers, 2012.

[SGC+14] Nicolás Serrano, Adrià Giménez, Jorge Civera, Alberto Sanchis, and Alfons Juan. Interactive handwriting recognition with limited user effort. *International Journal on Document Analysis and Recognition (IJDAR)*, 17(1):47–59, 2014.

[SHRM11] Rainer Simon, Bernhard Haslhofer, Werner Robitza, and Elaheh Momeni. Semantically Augmented Annotations in Digitized Map Collections. In *Proceedings of the 11th Annual International ACM/IEEE Joint Conference on Digital Libraries (JCDL '11)*, pages 199–202. ACM, 2011.

[SJSK14] Simon Scheider, Jim Jones, Alber Sánchez, and Carsten Keßler. Encoding and Querying Historic Map Content. In Joaquín Huerta, Sven Schade, and Carlos Granell, editors, *Connecting a Digital Europe Through Location and Place*, LNG&C, pages 251–273. Springer, 2014.

Bibliography

[SKO+11] Simon Scheider, Carsten Keßler, Jens Ortmann, Anusuriya Devaraju, Johannes Trame, Tomi Kauppinen, and Werner Kuhn. Semantic referencing of geosensor data and volunteered geographic information. In *Geospatial Semantics and the Semantic Web*, pages 27–59. Springer, 2011.

[SKP08] Pavlos Stathis, Ergina Kavallieratou, and Nikos Papamarkos. An Evaluation Survey of Binarization Algorithms on Historical Documents. In *Proceedings of the 19th International Conference on Pattern Recognition (ICPR '08)*, pages 1–4. IEEE, 2008.

[SMB11] Humphrey Southall, Ruth Mostern, and Merrick Lex Berman. On historical gazetteers. *International Journal of Humanities and Arts Computing*, 5(2):127–145, 2011.

[Smi07] Ray Smith. An Overview of the Tesseract OCR Engine. In *Proceedings of the 9th International Conference on Document Analysis and Recognition (ICDAR '07)*, pages 629–633. IEEE, 2007.

[Sou13] Humphrey Southall. Guest Editorial: Working Digitally with Historical Maps. *Journal of Map & Geography Libraries*, 9(1–2):1–7, 2013.

[SP12] Humphrey Southall and Petr Přidal. Old Maps Online: Enabling global access to historical mapping. *e-Perimetron*, 7(2):73–81, 2012.

[SPIB14] Rainer Simon, Peter Pilgerstorfer, Leif Isaksen, and Elton Barker. Towards semi-automatic annotation of toponyms on old maps. *e-Perimetron*, 9(3):105–112, 2014.

[SRGL00] Sharon Squire, Michael H. Ramsey, Michael J. Gardner, and Dustin Lister. Sampling proficiency test for the estimation of uncertainty in the spatial delineation of contamination. *Analyst*, 125:2026–2031, 2000.

[SSBD14] Shai Shalev-Shwartz and Shai Ben-David. *Understanding Machine Learning: From Theory to Algorithms*. Cambridge University Press, 2014.

[SSH13] Hendrik Schöneberg, Hans-Günter Schmidt, and Winfried Höhn. A Scalable, Distributed and Dynamic Workflow System for Digitization Processes. In *Proceedings of the 13th ACM/IEEE-CS Joint Conference on Digital Libraries (JCDL '13)*, pages 359–362. ACM, 2013.

[Ste05] Robert Louis Stevenson. *Essays in the Art of Writing*, page 117. Chatto & Windus, 1905.

[SU07] Andrew I. Schein and Lyle H. Ungar. Active Learning for Logistic Regression: an Evaluation. *Machine Learning*, 68(3):235–265, 2007.

[Tar75] Robert Endre Tarjan. Efficiency of a Good But Not Linear Set Union Algorithm. *Journal of the ACM*, 22(2):215–225, 1975.

[TDT13] Katayoun Torabi, Jessica Durgan, and Bryan Tarpley. Early Modern OCR Project (eMOP) at Texas A&M University: Using Aletheia to Train Tesseract. In *Proceedings of the 2013 ACM Symposium on Document Engineering (DocEng '13)*, pages 23–26. ACM, 2013.

[vA57] Hans-Joachim von Alberti. *Maß und Gewicht*. Akademie-Verlag Berlin, 1957.

[VD15] Arnaud Vandecasteele and Rodolphe Devillers. Improving Volunteered Geographic Information Quality Using a Tag Recommender System: The Case of OpenStreetMap. In Jamal Jokar Arsanjani, Alexander Zipf, Peter Mooney, and Marco Helbich, editors, *OpenStreetMap in GIScience*, LNG&C, pages 59–80. Springer, 2015.

[vEDF10] Martijn van Exel, Eduardo Dias, and Steven Fruijtier. The impact of crowdsourcing on spatial data quality indicators. In *Proceedings of the 6th International Conference on Geographic Information Science (GIScience '10)*. Springer, 2010.

[Vit67] Andrew J. Viterbi. Error bounds for convolutional codes and an asymptotically optimum decoding algorithm. *IEEE Transactions on Information Theory*, 13(2):260–269, 1967.

[vKW11] Marc van Kreveld and Lionov Wiratma. Median Trajectories Using Well-visited Regions and Shortest Paths. In *Proceedings of the 19th ACM SIGSPATIAL International Conference on Advances in Geographic Information Systems (ACM SIGSPATIAL '11)*, pages 241–250. ACM, 2011.

[WBB11] Kai Wang, Boris Babenko, and Serge Belongie. End-to-End Scene Text Recognition. In *Proceedings of the 2011 IEEE International Conference on Computer Vision (ICCV '11)*, pages 1457–1464. IEEE, 2011.

[WBKF14] Jerod J. Weinman, Zachary Butler, Dugan Knoll, and Jacqueline Feild. Toward Integrated Scene Text Reading. *IEEE Transactions on Pattern Analysis and Machine Intelligence*, 36(2):375–387, 2014.

[Wei13] Jerod Weinman. Toponym Recognition in Historical Maps by Gazetteer Alignment. In *Proceedings of the 12th International Conference on Document Analysis and Recognition (ICDAR '13)*, pages 1044–1048. IEEE, 2013.

[Whi13] Andrea P. White. X Marks the Spot: Extracting Data from Historical Maps to Locate Archaeological Sites. *Journal of Map & Geography Libraries*, 9(1–2):140–156, 2013.

[Win90] William E. Winkler. String Comparator Metrics and Enhanced Decision Rules in the Fellegi-Sunter Model of Record Linkage. In *Proceedings of the Section on Survey Research Methods*, pages 354–359. ASA, 1990.

Bibliography

[Woo07a] David Woodward.   Cartography and the Renaissance: Continuity and Change. In David Woodward, editor, *The History of Cartography*, volume 3, chapter 1, pages 3–24. University of Chicago Press, 2007.

[Woo07b] David Woodward. Techniques of Map Engraving, Printing, and Coloring in the European Renaissance. In David Woodward, editor, *The History of Cartography*, volume 3, chapter 22, pages 1172–1245. University of Chicago Press, 2007.

[WS06] Tasha Wade and Shelly Sommer. *A to Z GIS: An Illustrated Dictionary of Geographic Information Systems*. Esri Press, 2006.

[YLC16] Ronald Yu, Zexuan Luo, and Yao-Yi Chiang.   Recognizing Text in Historical Maps Using Maps from Multiple Time Periods.   In *23rd International Conference on Pattern Recognition (ICPR '16)*, pages 3993–3998. IEEE, 2016.

Figure Credits

The (modern) map sections in Figures 1.6, 6.1, 6.3, and 6.10 are based on data from Open-StreetMap, © OpenStreetMap contributors. For more information on the licensing, see http://www.openstreetmap.org/copyright

Some figures are licensed under Creative Commons (CC) licenses. For the respective license texts, see https://creativecommons.org/licenses/by-nc-sa/4.0/ and https://creativecommons.org/licenses/by-nc-nd/3.0/

All scans of historical maps by the Würzburg University Library used in this book can be found at http://franconica-online.de/

Acknowledgments

"I am told there are people who do not care for maps, and find it hard to believe."

— Robert Louis Stevenson [Ste05]

In the last three years, while working on this book, I was in the fortunate situation to be surrounded by people who indeed cared for maps. First and foremost, this holds for Dr. Thomas C. van Dijk, who supervised me and my research during this time. I would like to thank him for all his valuable advice (both on a scientific and personal level), his true interest in my work and research topic, his tireless helpfulness, his humor, and his optimism – in short, for being the best possible advisor one could hope for.

I would like to thank Prof. Dr. Alexander Wolff for being my senior advisor, having me at his chair, offering a pleasant and fruitful work environment, reviewing this thesis, and providing financial support. In addition, I thank Prof. Dr. Yao-Yi Chiang, who I got to know as an ardent promoter of the importance of digitizing historical maps, for reviewing this thesis.

The work presented in this book would not have been possible without support by the German Academic Scholarship Foundation (Studienstifung des deutschen Volkes), which provided a three-year research grant for this project. I am thankful for the generous financial support as well as for the various opportunities to meet young researchers from other disciplines.

The research presented in this book is joint work with several co-authors, whom I would like to thank for their valuable ideas and contributions. They are, in alphabetical order: Thomas C. van Dijk, Fabian Feitsch, Mauricio Giraldo Arteaga, Felix Kirchner, and Alexander Wolff. Beyond the direct contributors, I thank all of my colleagues at the Chair of Computer Science I as well as the University Library for their support and interest in my work.

All contributions in this book have been evaluated on real-world data, namely a variety of historical documents. This was only possible with the help of libraries maintaining collections of such documents. In this context, I would particularly like to thank Dr. Hans-Günter Schmidt of the Würzburg University Library for granting access to the precious maps of the *Franconica* collection. Furthermore, he helped by sharing his expertise, by providing practical use cases, and by financing part of this research through the Kallimachos project. Additional maps (as well as interesting use cases) were provided by the New York Public Library. There, I would especially like to thank the staff of the (now unfortunately discontinued) *Labs* department, in particular Mauricio Giraldo Arteaga, as well as Matthew Knutzen, for inviting me to New York City for two fruitful research visits.

While working on this book, I was in the founding and organizing committee of the *Exploring Old Maps (EOM)* workshop. Focusing on information extraction from histori-

157

Acknowledgments

cal maps, this workshop started as a joint cooperation of the Universities of Luxembourg and Würzburg. In Luxembourg, I would like to thank Prof. Dr. Christoph Schommer and Winfried Höhn for the pleasant collaboration.

I thank the Würzburg University Press (WUP), in particular Kristina Hanig and Claudia Schober, for taking care of the editing and publishing of the (physical) book you may hold in your hands.

Finally, I would like to cordially thank my family for their ongoing support and patience, particularly during the last months of finishing this book.

List of Publications

- B. Budig, T. C. van Dijk. **Journeys of the Past: A Hidden Markov Approach to Georeferencing Historical Itineraries.** In: *Proceedings of the 11th Workshop on Geographic Information Retrieval (GIR '17).* pp. 7:1–7:10. ACM (2017).

- B. Budig. **Exploring Local Geography for Toponym Matching.** In: *Proceedings of the 2nd International Workshop on Exploring Old Maps (EOM '17).* pp. 19–20. (2017).

- B. Budig, T. C. van Dijk, F. Feitsch, M. Giraldo Arteaga. **Polygon Consensus: Smart Crowdsourcing for Extracting Building Footprints from Historical Maps.** In: *Proceedings of the 24th ACM SIGSPATIAL International Conference on Advances in Geographic Information Systems (ACM SIGSPATIAL '16).* pp. 66:1–66:4. ACM (2016).

- B. Budig, T. C. van Dijk, F. Kirchner. **Glyph Miner: A System for Efficiently Extracting Glyphs from Early Prints in the Context of OCR.** In: *Proceedings of the 16th ACM/IEEE-CS Joint Conference on Digital Libraries (JCDL '16).* pp. 31–34. ACM (2016).

- B. Budig. **Towards a Pipeline for Metadata Extraction from Historical Maps.** In: *Proceedings of the 1st International Workshop on Exploring Old Maps (EOM '16).* (2016).

- B. Budig. **Efficient Algorithms and User Interaction for Metadata Extraction from Historical Maps.** In: *Proceedings of the 2nd ACM SIGSPATIAL PhD Workshop.* pp. 4:1–4:4. ACM (2016).

- B. Budig, T. C. van Dijk, A. Wolff. **Matching Labels and Markers in Historical Maps: an Algorithm with Interactive Postprocessing.** In: *Transactions on Spatial Algorithms and Systems (TSAS).* 2, 13:1–13:24. ACM (2016). Included in the *Annual Best of Computing – Notable Books and Articles 2016* list by the ACM Computing Review.

- L. Beckmann, B. Budig, T. C. van Dijk, J. Schamel. **There and Back Again: Using Fréchet-Distance Diagrams to Find Trajectory Turning Points.** In: *Proceedings of the 23rd ACM SIGSPATIAL International Conference on Advances in Geographic Information Systems (ACM SIGSPATIAL '15).* pp. 238–241. ACM (2015). Best Poster Award Runners-up.

List of Publications

- B. Budig, T. C. van Dijk. **Active Learning for Classifying Template Matches in Historical Maps.** In: *Proceedings of the 18th International Conference on Discovery Science (DS '15).* pp. 33–47. Springer (2015). Best Applied Paper Award.

- B. Budig, T. C. van Dijk, A. Wolff. **Matching Labels and Markers in Historical Maps: an Algorithm with Interactive Postprocessing.** In: *Proceedings of the 2nd ACM SIGSPATIAL International Workshop on MapInteraction (MapInteract '14).* pp. 22–28. ACM (2014).

- J.-H. Haunert, B. Budig. **An Algorithm for Map Matching Given Incomplete Road Data.** In: *Proceedings of the 20th ACM SIGSPATIAL International Conference on Advances in Geographic Information Systems (ACM SIGSPATIAL '12).* pp. 510–513. ACM (2012).

www.ingramcontent.com/pod-product-compliance
Lightning Source LLC
La Vergne TN
LVHW080117070326
832902LV00015B/2629